D0065081

JAIME ESCALANTE

Sensational Teacher

Ann Byers

Enslow Publishers, Inc.
40 Industrial Road   PO Box 38
Box 398   Aldershot
Berkeley Heights, NJ 07922   Hants GU12 6BP
USA   UK
http://www.enslow.com

Library of Congress Cataloging-in-Publication Data

Byers, Ann.
      Jaime Escalante : sensational teacher / Ann Byers.
         p. cm. — (Hispanic biographies)
      Includes bibliographical references and index.
      Summary: Presents the life of the Bolivian-born teacher who immigrated to the
United States where he inspired and motivated his inner city students to excel in
mathematics.
      ISBN 0-89490-763-8
      1. Escalante. Jaime—Juvenile literature. 2. Mathematics
teachers—California—Biography—Juvenile literature. 3. Hispanic American
mathematics teachers—California—Biography—Juvenile literature.
      [1. Escalante, Jaime. 2. Teachers. 3. Hispanic Americans—Biography.] I. Title.
II. Series.
QA29.E73B94   1996
510' .92—dc20   95-50071
[B]   CIP
                                                      AC

Printed in the United States of America

10 9 8 7 6

Illustration Credits: Ann Byers, pp. 7 , 9, 73; Courtesy of Jaime Escalante, pp. 15, 23,
26, 28, 29, 31, 38, 39, 40, 44, 46, 64, 89, 100, 102, 104, 106, 110, 113, 115.

Cover Illustration: Courtesy of Jaime Escalante

CONTENTS

THE KEY

So far, nothing had worked with this class. For Jaime Escalante, mathematics was wonderfully logical, full of interesting patterns, and, above all, very practical. It was the language of science, engineering, and computers. It opened the doors to high-paying jobs. But these high-school students were so turned off to school, so accustomed to low expectations of themselves, that they seemed to tolerate his class only a little more than their other classes. He was determined to find a way to motivate them to want to learn, to try to achieve.

So, on this day he was wearing a cook's apron and hat. The students took notice as they entered the room. When he arranged several apples wordlessly on a cutting board laid across his desk, they were mildly amused. When he produced a razor-sharp meat cleaver, they were ready to listen. When he hacked the first apple to pieces in a matter of seconds, they were too stunned not to be fully attentive.

Dramatically he sliced the remaining apples—into fourths, thirds, fifths, eighths—and distributed them to the students who were now, in spite of themselves, positively fascinated by the tangible demonstration of the abstract concept of fractions.

"What do you have?" he asked one student after another. "How much?"

They had different amounts: one half, three fourths, one sixth.

"How about you?" he challenged one student. "How much do you have?"

The boy studied the piece of fruit before responding hesitantly. "Two thirds," he ventured.

"Too slow," the teacher corrected, taking a bite. "Now you only have one half."[1]

Escalante had many tricks for motivating learning, most of which he created himself. He used a Coke can that sported sunglasses and earphones as it rocked back and forth and made noises to capture a class's attention. He wired lights around a circular board and

Jaime Escalante's unique teaching style includes personalized instruction and many creative incentives.

flashed them in a game that helped students recall trigonometric functions. A similar, triangular light board taught vectors.[2] He devised a time clock with time cards that students used to punch in and out of class and after-school study periods. Since he paid them a penny an hour, they eagerly and quickly figured out how to calculate, add, and multiply fractions of an hour.

He passed out candy on test days to encourage good attendance and challenged boys to handball games: If the student won, he got an "A"; if the teacher won, the student did his homework. The teacher never lost.[3]

Escalante knew this kind of motivation could only take his students so far. What would they do when they left his class, when they were no longer in school and there were no clever tricks, stimulating toys, or teasing encouragements to do better? He had to find a way to move them from external incentives to inward desire. They needed to want to do well because of something within themselves.

They all had some kind of longing somewhere deep inside. But for many of these children of the *barrios* of East Los Angeles—the low-income, Mexican-American ghettos of the inner city—the fragile flame of a dream had been all but snuffed out by an urban environment that offered little. Their world consisted of crowded apartments, blue-collar jobs, early pregnancies, gangs, and drugs. What kind of expectations were realistic for them? What hope was worth the effort? He had to give them something to reach for that would awaken the tiny spark within them of a desire to achieve.

He found that something in the Advanced Placement (A.P.) calculus exam. This was a college-level math test for high-school students. Anyone who passed the exam earned three, four, or five units of college credit, depending on the test score. The A.P. calculus test was so difficult that less

E scalante's classroom walls are covered with encouraging and motivational posters, including his prominently displayed "Ganas: That's all you need" motto.

than 2 percent of all the students in the country even tried to take it.[4] It was just the kind of challenge these kids needed to force them to dig deep inside themselves and find a reason to try. It would put them on the same team with him; instead of students against teacher, it would be teacher and students together against a giant enemy.

First, though, he would have to create that motivation. He began by outlining his expectations. They were going to work, he told them. They were going to work harder than they ever had before.

There would be no free rides, no excuses. Each class would begin with a quiz, and a test would be given every Friday. Although school started at 8:00 A.M., Escalante's class began at 7:30 A.M. He would open the doors at 7:00 A.M. and they would be on time. And, he told them, they would pass the exam.

Then he delivered the heart of his lecture: "The only thing I ask from you is *ganas*—desire." He had the Spanish word blazoned on a large poster and displayed prominently on the classroom wall: "*Ganas* . . . That's All You Need."

"*Ganas* conquers all," he declared. "With *ganas* we will learn to overcome any obstacle. It is all you need to succeed in my class."

He ended his speech with the unique blend of bluster and humor and taunting his students would come to expect from him: "If you don't have the *ganas*, I will give it to you because I am the expert!"[5]

THIRD-
GENERATION
TEACHER

![star icon] It was only natural that Jaime Escalante would become a teacher. His father and mother and mother's father were all teachers.

In the South American country of Bolivia in the 1920s, teachers worked where the government assigned them. Most began their careers in low-paying positions in small schools far from any major city. More than half the people of Bolivia lived in rural areas with very few conveniences and spoke their own languages rather than the Spanish that was used in the cities. Zenobio and Sara Escalante had been placed in the remote Aymara village of Achacachi, high in the Andes Mountains near the shores of Lake Titicaca.

The couple had adjusted to the simple life of this village until Sara realized she was expecting her second child. She did not want him to be born in this place so far from any doctor or medicine or female relative. As the time of the baby's arrival drew closer, Sara made the bumpy, four-hour trip down the dirt roads of the mountain to the city of La Paz, where she had family. On December 31, 1930, she gave birth to her first son, her second child, and christened him Jaime Alfonso Escalante Gutiérrez—"Escalante" for his father, Zenobio, and "Gutiérrez" for his mother's father, José.

Jaime spent the first years of his life in Achacachi. He was an active, energetic child who was always looking for new adventures, very often devising his own. He played with his sisters and little brother in the dirt patio of their tiny, three-room house and freely roamed the open fields and the few shops of the little village plaza. He loved all kinds of sports, especially handball. He did not attend school, but his grandfather taught him to read and to count. On their frequent outings, the retired teacher kept Jaime's young mind racing to solve riddles, spell words, and create games.

His pleasant, carefree world was shaken when he was nine years old and his parents separated. His mother moved with her children from their quiet home in the mountains, where life revolved around a single village square, to La Paz, the largest city in all Bolivia.[1] It felt terribly crowded—teeming with people and spilling over with cars. Building after building lined the mazes of cobblestone streets that crisscrossed the city. Everyone spoke Spanish, sounds that were foreign to Jaime's ears, accustomed as they were to the Aymara language.

The greatest jolt came when Jaime began his formal education. He discovered that children were expected not only to sit still, but at attention in class. They had to raise their hands before speaking. They had to be on time and follow the teachers' rules. He was not used to so much discipline.

Adjusting to the classroom structure was not the most difficult change for Jaime. He felt terribly out of place. His clothing was very different from that of his classmates and the children on the playground could not understand the language he spoke. "Look at this kid," the children laughed. "He's wearing sandals. Look at his jacket. It's an Indian jacket. Indian! Indian! Indian!" they jeered.

As soon as his mother could afford to buy him new clothes, Jaime discarded his Aymara garments. He replaced his sandals with shoes borrowed from a relative every morning and returned every afternoon after school. He picked up Spanish quickly.

Jaime soon won over the boys at school with his exceptional athletic abilities. Handball was his favorite sport, but Jaime was also good at soccer and basketball. His friends played for the enjoyment of the game; Jaime competed for the thrill of winning.[2]

As a schoolteacher, Sara Escalante was not well paid. There were days when she had very little—once only one slice of bread—to divide among her two daughters and three sons.[3] So there was no money to spend on children's toys. Jaime was used to creating his own amusements.

He watched other boys riding bicycles and decided to build something similar for himself. He attached wheels to a piece of board and, with his younger sister Bertha behind him, rolled down the hilly streets of his neighborhood as fast as any of his friends did on bicycles. His "truck" had an advantage over theirs: In the winter, he could remove the wheels and coast down the ice-covered slopes of Chacaltaya, outside the city.[4]

In La Paz, handball games were played for money, so Jaime would not squander the precious *pesos* (Spanish coins) needed to play by buying balls when he could make them himself. He stripped the rubber from old tires and heated it until he could wrap it tightly around a stone.[5]

He fashioned all his own tools. He crafted knives and saws and screwdrivers from iron bars retrieved

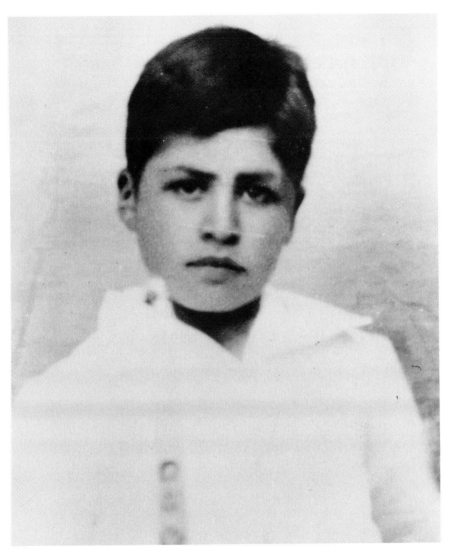

As a child, Jaime Escalante was creative as well as mischievous. Above is Escalante at age seven.

from construction sites. He heated them in an open fire and pounded them until they were flat and sharp. He made hammers of nearly every size. The heads were attached to the handles with leather pieces cut from the tops and sides of worn-out shoes. His tools were crude and they may have looked odd, but they probably worked as well as anything bought in a store.

The raw materials for all his inventions could be found in his neighbors' discards. Jaime used to take the truck he had made from house to house. "Do you have anything to throw away?" he would ask.[6]

Often the ladies of the houses were glad to give him a peso or two to haul away what they no longer wanted. The few coins did not amount to very much, but to Jaime's imaginative mind, the objects the women put in his homemade cart were of far greater value. They could be taken apart and the pieces recombined to create dozens of toys, games, equipment, and furnishings. The possibilities were endless. He kept what appeared promising and threw the rest away.

Sara became upset as Jaime's piles of treasure grew. He had shoes and boards and scraps of material all over the house—in every corner and under the beds. "I can't clean around this junk," his mother complained. "There are spiders in it."

"Mom," Jaime protested, "this is not junk. This is money."[7]

Even though he was able to make almost everything he needed or wanted, Jaime found that some pesos were necessary, especially for wagers for the handball games he loved so much. He developed a number of profitable skills when he was still a young child. He learned to make and repair shoes, to sew clothes, to cut hair, and to use carpentry tools. Sometimes he worked for the tailor who lived across the street, sewing buttons on sweaters for ten cents a button.

One Sunday when Jaime was eleven years old, he was not allowed to go out because of some misdeed he had committed. The tailor had a forty-button job for him, but Jaime could not leave his house. Jaime's older sister, Olimpia, brought the clothing and the buttons to her troublesome but industrious brother. When the task was finished, the tailor gave his employee two dollars.

"Why only two dollars?" Jaime wanted to know. Forty buttons should have earned him four dollars.

The tailor said that some of the work had been poor. He had had to resew some of the buttons.

"I want to see the ones you redid," Jaime challenged. "My work is first class, and I don't think any were bad."

He was sure the tailor was lying, but the man still refused to pay him the full amount.

"If you don't give me the other two dollars," Jaime warned, "I'll make you pay a different way."

The tailor reported the threat to Sara. Jaime knew he would never see the money he had rightfully earned. Although his mother tried to end the matter, Jaime looked for a way to get back at his employer.

He waited a few days, allowing the tailor to think he had forgotten the incident. Then he used his homemade saw to cut a large board from some scrap lumber. On it he painted, in large letters, "Out of Business." In the middle of a Friday night, while the entire neighborhood slept, he nailed the sign above the window of the tailor's shop. The weekend was over before the tailor realized why he had no customers and on Monday he had to patch the holes the extra-large nails had made in his wall. Jaime ended up spending more than the two dollars he had lost as well as suffering the wrath of his mother.[8]

It was no wonder that Olimpia, two years older than Jaime, lectured him nearly every morning and prayed aloud that he would not get into trouble that day. She knew the many mischievous things he did at home and all the pranks he played at school. He confided in her and she covered for him. In exchange for her help, Jaime would have to eat whatever food their mother served that she did not like.[9]

For example, when the children had report cards to show their mother, Olimpia put hers—with the good grades—on top, Bertha's on the bottom, and Jaime's sandwiched in between.

"Here, Mom," she would say. "This is my report card. Sign it here. And here. And this is Bertha's; sign it here."[10]

Jaime believed that the only reason his report cards were not good was that his teachers were not able to keep his inquisitive mind busy with challenging work. He could not sit still with nothing on which to focus his thoughts and energies. If he did not think an assignment was constructive, he would create his own project—and the teachers usually did not approve of the projects he thought up.

One of his elementary-school teachers, Umberto Bilbao, discovered the key that brought attention to his lessons, discipline to his study habits, and enthusiasm to his schoolwork: mathematics. Bilbao had given him a rectangular card.

"Jaime," he said, indicating two corners of the card. "This point and this point are opposite. If you draw a line connecting them, the points are called vertexes and the line is a diagonal."

He instructed his pupil to cut another card from a piece of heavy paper and see how many diagonals he could draw on it. The assignment took him only a few minutes.

"How many did you get?" the teacher asked.

"Four."

Bilbao was patient. "I don't think you understand, Jaime."

Jaime was sure of his answer. He showed his teacher the card on which his two diagonals had formed an "X."

"Look," Jaime demonstrated. "One, two"—and, turning the card over—"three, four."

"You're a smart kid," Bilbao acknowledged. "You're going to start learning fractions."[11]

Jaime already had an idea of what fractions were all about. He had watched his mother introduce the topic in her afternoon classes. In fact, Jaime learned the fresh fruit method he used later with his own students from Sara Escalante. She had drafted him to help her carry about twenty-five oranges to school. Sara not only sliced the fruit into various-size wedges, but she also cut a band of peel from around the middle of an orange. Holding the band in a flat line, she said of the length, "This is the circumference."

"And this"—the straight line across the top of a wedge—"is the diameter. Let's see how many times the diameter goes into the circumference. One, two, three," she measured. "And a little bit left over. We're going to call this 'pi.'" Jaime thought she was a good teacher.

Jaime learned another, more essential, concept from his mother. He says the importance of ganas originated with her. When she asked for his help bringing the oranges to school, he complained. His classes were held in the morning and now she wanted him to go to school again in the afternoon with her. He did not want to. Besides, the oranges were heavy and he was little.

Sara lit into him: "You don't have *ganas* to help me out? No? Well, you're going to have *ganas* because I'm going to give you *ganas* right now!"[12]

ADOLESCENCE

By the time he was in eighth grade, Jaime had surpassed his mother's mathematical knowledge. She had shown him concepts and taught him to memorize rules, but he understood the patterns beneath the concepts and developed shortcuts around the rules. Sara realized that her son was exceptionally bright, even if too mischievous.[1] Although children were not required to attend school beyond the primary grades, Jaime's mother sacrificed in order for him to attend one of the best secondary schools in Bolivia. When he was fourteen, in 1945, she enrolled

Eighteen-year-old Jaime Escalante poses with his friend Victor on school grounds.

him in San Calixto, a school founded and operated by Jesuit priests.

It was here that Jaime discovered the marvels of chemistry and physics and higher mathematics. He gave these teachers his unwavering attention. He read far ahead in his math books, finishing all the problems in the final chapters months before his classmates even started them. He devoured his older sister's chemistry books and his cousin's physics texts before the subjects were even introduced by his teachers. He borrowed books from his instructors and volunteered to clean the science laboratory so he could explore the wonders of the lab's motors, weights, machines, and other fascinating devices.[2]

Subjects such as history, language, and religion could not hold his interest. He looked for ways to avoid these subjects—or at least slice fifteen minutes from them!

The clock that monitored the school bells was located in a tower above the second story. On several occasions, usually on days history tests were given, Jaime unlocked the door to the stairs with a key he had made and slipped up unnoticed. If anyone caught him, he would tell them the door had been left open and he was cleaning the clock so it would not rust from the Bolivian rains. What he actually did was grease the clock's massive minute hand. Then he crept down, making sure to be in his classroom before a quarter past the hour. That was the moment at which the force of gravity pulled the lubricated hand down to the half past position. On those days, the bell rang fifteen minutes early.

After about a month, the vice principal figured things out and Jaime was suspended for a week.[3]

Frequently, he could avoid some of the classes he disliked by arriving late. All five doors to the building were locked as soon as the morning bell rang—except the door to the main office. Anyone entering that door after 8:00 A.M. received automatic detention. That was not a problem for Jaime. He simply made keys for each door.

One morning a teacher blocked the way to his class, so he ducked into a restroom. He did not remember that the school was on a special schedule that day. When the bell sounded unexpectedly, he wondered if someone had been greasing the clock. He came out of his hiding place, but by then the students were seated and the hallways empty.

"What are you doing here?" his teacher demanded. "All the doors are closed. How did you get in?"

He could not very well say that he had come at 8:00 and had been in the restroom for two hours. The incident ended like many others: a few days' suspension and an uncle or cousin pleading with the priests to accept him back.[4] Sara had long since reached her limit and had refused to be amused by his

Jaime's cousin Fernando was a Franciscan priest. Fernando was one of the many family members who advocated for Jaime with the school principal.

jokes and pranks or to intervene with teachers or principals to soften the punishment his actions earned him.[5]

The worst thing Jaime did in high school was more a reaction than an intentional act. It happened when a teacher from France began criticizing Bolivia, striking his desk repeatedly with a piece of wood to emphasize his points. Jaime's face registered his disagreement with the instructor's tirade. The teacher, who was already agitated, yelled at him and hurled the piece of wood at him. The smack of the wood on his chest so startled Jaime that he reached for the nearest available object to return the volley. The closest thing happened to be an ink bottle and Jaime was an excellent pitcher. The Frenchman marched him to the dean's office and then went home to change his once-white shirt.[6]

After high school, young Bolivian men were required to serve in the army, so in 1950 Jaime began a brief military adventure. The country seemed to be in a never-ending state of civil war. In Jaime's nineteen years, Bolivia had been governed by nine different presidents, all but one of whom had been either killed or overthrown or both. When Jaime entered the service, Bolivian communists were stirring up rebellion in several towns and cities, inciting strikes in factories and riots in the streets.

Jaime was not interested in the political ideologies of the conflict. His main concern in the military was

Jaime Escalante (in center, looking up) at his high school graduation from San Calixto.

obtaining good food. Rations in the army were limited to bread and coffee in the morning and a bowl of soup in the afternoon.[7] The meats and cheeses and vegetables in the shops and restaurants of the countryside were a hundred times better than the meager military provisions. Jaime, with the help of a good friend, plotted ways to get some of the tasty food "on the outside."

Together they collected items the soldiers did not use: extra soap, toothpaste, matches. These were in short supply in war-torn areas, so they were able to trade the goods easily for the agricultural bounty of

E scalante (on right) with an army buddy and some friends. During his time in the army, Escalante used his ingenuity to obtain good meals for himself instead of eating army provisions.

the villages. They were careful to bring back enough food to satisfy the soldiers who had given up their surplus goods.

One day Jaime and his friend wrote an official-looking note stating that the two servicemen bearing the letter were assigned the responsibility of going to a nearby village to inspect ammunition. They did go to the village, but all they inspected were the local restaurants. When they returned at 6:00 P.M., they had only one cent between them. When their comrades asked how the inspection went, they told them that everything was fine. After that, they volunteered for any inspections that came up.

Jaime's time in the army was not all a lighthearted pursuit of pleasure. A real war was going on, one of the many revolutions that rocked the country regularly. Jaime did see military action. His most vivid memory of that time was of an incident that occurred as he was sitting with other soldiers from his battalion in a town, eating. He looked up to see an ambulance speeding toward them. One by one, wounded people were carried from the ambulance, so many he thought the line would never stop. That was when the reality of the danger of his situation hit him. "This is what may be waiting for me," he thought. "I have no idea if I will come back alive." It was the first time he had felt real fear.

The fear seemed to melt away in the excitement of combat. When he fought, Jaime had to put the image of the parade of bleeding men out of his mind. He did not fight much, however. The battles were few and brief. The revolt was small and not very well organized; it was easily put to rest by the government forces, and Jaime was discharged early.[8]

When he returned from his military obligation, he was ready to abandon the practical jokes of his youth and begin serious consideration of life. Jaime's father had died when he was fourteen and his mother could not afford to send all her five children to school. So

Escalante (bottom right) rides the train with some members of his troop. This was the typical mode of transportation.

Jaime looked around for the easiest and quickest path to a career.

He enrolled in college, intending to study business. When that failed to be a challenge or even to be interesting, he switched his major to engineering. The engineering teachers presented nothing that excited him, so he dropped out, discouraged.

A brief encounter with a friend in 1951 set him on a different course[9]—a path that would take him to a profession that would demand all of his resources, that would challenge every fiber of his emotions as well as his intellect, that would fit his personality wonderfully, and that would reward him beyond anything he could even imagine.

A GOAL ...
AND SUCCESS

Escalante's friend was going to become a teacher. In fact, the day they met, Roberto was going to take the entrance exam for Normal Superior, the college that prepared students for teaching careers. He talked Escalante into joining him.[1] After all, it took six years to become an engineer and only four to become a teacher. No one was surprised when Escalante scored the highest of all the applicants on the physics and math tests given that day.

During his first year at Normal Superior, Escalante met an old friend: Umberto Bilbao, the teacher who had recognized and nurtured his mathematical talent ten years earlier. Escalante's elementary-school teacher was now a college professor, instructing another generation of teachers on how to inspire their students to understand vertexes, diagonals, and fractions.

By Escalante's second year at Normal Superior, Bilbao had advanced to a very high position and was responsible for schools throughout the country. He took a special interest in Escalante and observed that he possessed more than mathematical skills. He had also become an excellent electrician and demonstrated tremendous creativity. Bilbao asked his student to help in some of the workshops he conducted. Once he invited Escalante to assist him in a large presentation he was making for a nationwide conference. He needed Escalante's electrical expertise and he wanted his protégé to be exposed to the latest in educational technology.[2]

In the middle of that year, Bilbao encountered a problem that he would turn into an opportunity for his former pupil. At the Instituto Americano, a physics teacher had died suddenly and a competent substitute could not be found. Bilbao went to the teaching college, Normal Superior, looking for four last-year students to take over the deceased teacher's four classes. But four senior students able to teach physics could not be found. Bilbao approached Escalante.[3]

After all, he had come from a top-notch Jesuit school with a strong background in the sciences. He was experienced in using the laboratory. So, while three older, more advanced Normal Superior students substituted in the first-, second-, and third-year classes, Escalante—with barely more than one year of college and no actual instruction in how to teach—taught the fourth-year students.[4]

Escalante's busyness—with the extracurricular workshops and his substitute teaching assignment—gave him as good an excuse as he needed to "ditch" the classes he considered dull. In the ten months that constituted a year at Normal Superior, he attended classes a total of only one or two weeks. His instructors took all of his activities into account. They gave him extra work to make up for some of his absences and allowed him to take the final exams.

When the half-year substitute assignment ended, Bilbao had another proposition for his fledgling teacher. The government was building a new boys' high school and it needed teachers. (In Bolivia, boys went to boys' schools and girls went to girls' schools.)

Escalante's initial response was negative. For one thing, he was still a student—a student with no formal training as yet in teaching techniques. For another, his attendance record was abysmally poor. Bilbao, however, wanted him to teach and Escalante loved a challenge. So, at age twenty-one, Escalante accepted his first real teaching position.

This new adventure proved to be one of the most difficult he had attempted. The brand-new school had no students. Since attendance in secondary school was not mandatory, the teachers were given the task of going to the primary schools and convincing the students that they needed to continue their education beyond the junior-high level. They went from school to school to lure boys to high school in general and to their classrooms in particular. They pointed out the advantages of a school in their neighborhood, close to home.

Because recruitment was slow, Escalante and the physical education teacher devised a plan for expanding their campaign beyond the junior highs to boys who were already enrolled in other high schools. They bought several soccer balls and approached prospective students.

"We have a new school where all we do is play futbol [soccer]," they teased. "The only grades we give are A's. Anybody want to play futbol?"

They began with six boys. Before long, twenty came, then twenty-five. By the time a principal arrived, the Villarroel School had sixty boys in attendance. They did play a lot of ball, but they also had lessons in between their games and tournaments.

Villarroel was a very poor school. The families whose children attended did not have money, and the government provided little beyond the lunches of bread, cheese, and milk and the tiny staff of three teachers and one principal. There were no textbooks, so Escalante taught from his high-school notes, sharing the tricks, secrets, and shortcuts that he had discovered in math.

Teaching at Villarroel, Escalante probably gained more insight into how to motivate teenagers and inspire learning than he ever would at Normal Superior. Some of the techniques he would find useful thirty and forty years later he developed there. He attracted students with sports and then hooked them on math. He promised them A's, but made them work for them. When the class's work began to lag, he demanded after-school sessions. He pushed them hard and saw them succeed.[5]

When college began the next year, Escalante had an emergency teaching credential that allowed him to teach while he was completing his college work. He was still at Villarroel, and Bilbao offered him a second job: teaching physics at Bolivar High School in the afternoons. If he was to continue in teaching, he needed to graduate, so he remained enrolled in college. At first he saw little reason to attend classes—he had simply taken and passed the tests the previous year.

Then he met Fabiola Tapia. She was also studying to become a teacher, and she was intrigued with the

Escalante (left) always had an interest in sports. Besides teaching physics at Bolivar High School, he also coached the school's volleyball team.

unusual ways Jaime figured out his mathematics problems. One of her friends was struggling in math, and she asked Jaime to show them his special techniques.

"You have a funny way of doing things," she smiled.[6] Jaime only helped her once or twice, but it was enough to begin a friendship. Two years later, when he was twenty-three and she was twenty-one, they married. The same year, 1954, he earned his college degree.[7]

Before Escalante graduated from Normal Superior, however, and before he earned his official teaching

*J*aime Escalante and Fabiola Tapia were married in 1954.

credential, he fulfilled what had been a dream ever since he began to pursue a career in education: He was invited to teach physics at San Calixto, his old school. This was a private school—one of the best. It was the scene of many of his adolescent pranks, but also the site of great adventures for him in science and higher mathematics. The offer meant that his reputation was changing from that of a troublemaker to that of a respected professional. He accepted eagerly.

Escalante (second from right) joined in welcoming Bolivian president, Hernan Siles Zuazo, to San Calixto.

Even the responsibility of explaining atomic numbers and theories of thermodynamics to scores of high-school students was not enough to keep Escalante's sharp mind and restless body occupied. So, although he taught at San Calixto in the mornings and at Bolivar in the afternoons, he spent evenings tutoring students privately or teaching at the police academy. That still left him weekends for outings with Fabiola and their son, Jaimito.

After eight years, he interrupted his hectic pace when he accepted an invitational scholarship for Latin

American teachers offered by the United States. He spent a year in San Juan, Puerto Rico, a United States territory, with industrial arts and science instructors from other Spanish-speaking countries.[8] The courses were interesting and the environment stimulating, but Escalante still found himself with plenty of free time. So when he discovered that his intelligent, educated colleagues did not know how to mend their clothes, sew on a button, or iron their pants—all skills he had acquired as a child—he set up a weekend business and supplemented the small allowance that came with his scholarship.[9] Escalante enjoyed the year in Puerto Rico and the brief visit to the United States that concluded it, but he was very happy to be back in La Paz, back in the classroom.

Early in his teaching career, Escalante developed and demonstrated the principle that would become his lifelong creed and his students' daily challenge:

DETERMINATION—after his first exposure at Villarroel, Escalante was determined to become a good teacher; he had tapped into a powerful ganas;

plus DISCIPLINE—to prepare his lessons, he had to forego the handball courts and other pleasures;

plus HARD WORK—he never held fewer than three jobs at a time, sometimes four;

equals SUCCESS—Escalante had a good income, a happy family, a comfortable lifestyle, and work he enjoyed.

DETERMINATION

Fabiola kept pressing Jaime. "You're not going to succeed over here," she warned. "The political situation is getting worse."

Bolivia had always been wracked by political upheaval and civil unrest. In the 126 years from its independence in 1825 to its largest revolution in 1952, the country went through 179 changes of government.[1] The instability that churned throughout Bolivia's history had intensified in the 1950s and 1960s. Different groups fought for control of the government and the people were seldom sure who actually held power.

Governmental instability had created economic chaos. Victor Paz Estenssoro, president after the revolution of 1952, put most of the nation's tin mines, which generated the bulk of the country's wealth, under government control. The price of tin on the world market remained drastically low for the next two decades and inflation steadily rose, squeezing the lifeblood from the entire economy. Government officials tried desperately to prop up the crumbling economy. They laid off many workers and refused to raise the wages of others to keep pace with rampant inflation. By 1960, everyone was feeling the pinch. The average annual income for each person was the equivalent of one hundred American dollars.[2] Teachers' salaries were so low and prices so high that Escalante's multiple jobs were necessary just to feed his family. "There is no future for you here," Fabiola kept telling her husband.

Escalante knew his wife wanted to go to America. She was genuinely concerned about conditions in Bolivia, and besides, her brothers, uncles, and other family members were in the United States. Her father had earned his college degree in California and had encouraged his sons to do the same. The letters that came from the United Stated described a land of peace and security and opportunity. "In America," she told him, "is everything you need."[3]

At first, Escalante refused. He had built a kitchen onto their small house and they were comfortable. He

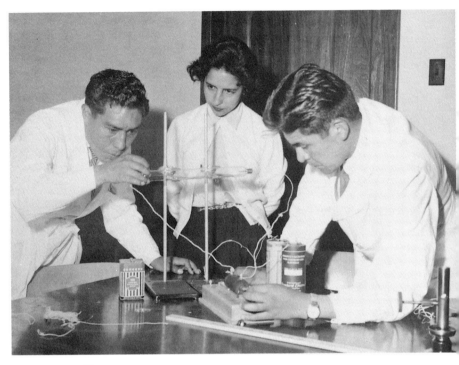

E scalante (on right) trained physics teachers in Bolivia.

had a car—an old one, but still it was more than many Bolivians were able to afford. He had students who responded to his inspirational challenges and colleagues who respected his abilities. He was educating future leaders and thought this was a valuable contribution to his country. He did not need anything.

Fabiola was persistent. She tried to make him see the growing distrust between Bolivia and the United States. He had spent a year in Puerto Rico, an

American territory, financed by the American government, she reminded him. People were likely to focus attention on him, call him a Yankee sympathizer, and he could be a victim of the next revolt.[4]

When he realized how much she wanted to go, he relented. Her brother, Sam Tapia, lived in Pasadena, on the eastern edge of Los Angeles, California. He agreed to sponsor them and he pledged to support them financially until they could take care of themselves. They filled out the immigration papers and sold everything they owned. Jaime said good-bye to his family and friends, telling them he was going to America to begin a new life—starting from zero. Fabiola and Jaimito would stay in Bolivia with family members while he settled and found a job. Then he would send for them.

So he flew the forty-five hundred miles from La Paz to Los Angeles alone. He stepped off the plane on the last day of the year, 1963—his thirty-third birthday.

Tapia had warned Escalante that two things were important in the United States. One was transportation. "Over here," his brother-in-law explained, "we measure distance as a function of time." People defined the distance from Los Angeles to San Diego, for example, not as 130 miles but as two and a half hours. "You have to have

While Fabiola and Jaimito temporarily remained in Bolivia, Jaime Escalante moved to the United States. This is the photo from his passport.

transportation," he insisted. "And the second thing," he continued, "is the language. You need to learn to speak English."[5]

The first was easy. Escalante paid $2,400 of the $3,000 he had brought to help him get established for a brand-new Volkswagen "beetle,"[6] a car he would drive for more than twenty years.

The second was another matter. The English language was nothing like either the Spanish or the Aymara tongues. He found it much more difficult to learn a language at age thirty-three than it had been at nine.

Someone told him that he might learn English by watching television news. That sounded like a good idea. The first stories he saw discouraged him. He could understand without any words that they were about a bank robbery on one side of the city and a shooting on the other. This was his picture of life in America.

Tapia suggested he try focusing on the editorials because the commentators spoke especially well. Escalante paid attention as the news reporters gave their opinions, but there were no pictures to help him comprehend. The more he listened, the more difficult the language seemed.

Escalante found out that the YMCA had English tutors. That seemed like a solution: some one-on-one help. It was the way he would bring a slower physics student up to the level of his peers. Escalante's tutor, however, turned out to be a man from Europe with an accent that sometimes confused even native English speakers![7]

Escalante could not afford to wait until he mastered the language before getting a job. His brother-in-law had not been able to find work for him, so he set out himself, armed with little English but a lot of determination.

In the end, his ganas paid off. Mr. Polsky at Van de Kamp's Coffee Shop needed someone to sweep and mop and arrange chairs—and that did not require any language skills. So the renowned Bolivian physics teacher became a janitor.

The job came with a uniform—shirt, pants, and special shoes. Escalante cringed inside as he tied an apron around his waist. He never thought starting from zero would mean wearing an apron and scrubbing floors. It felt like a punishment,[8] but options for a non-English speaker were few. If he wanted to advance, this was where he had to start.

He did not have to stay in this position, Escalante reminded himself. He would learn the language. Once he had the language, he would get a different job. Eventually he would move up.

More determined than ever to conquer English, Escalante decided to plunge into it full force by enrolling at Pasadena City College, a block away from the coffee shop. He worked only eight or nine hours at Van de Kamp's, six days a week, so he had plenty of time for school. After all, he was used to working three or four jobs at one time. His brother-in-law went with him to the admissions office.

Entry to the junior college required a placement test in a major field of study. Escalante knew physics backwards and forwards, but he would not be able to demonstrate that on an exam written in English. Tapia asked for the math test because it would present the least language problem.

The admissions employee had no encouraging smile. He explained brusquely that the test would take two hours and he would answer no questions during that time. Tapia translated and Escalante began.

Escalante's brother-in-law had made a wise choice. As much as the new immigrant stumbled in English, he was exceptionally fluent in the language of math. His pencil danced rapidly across the pages and in twenty-five minutes he approached the man who was administering the test.

Now the man was angry. "I told you, 'No questions!'" he raged. "This is why we don't want to give tests to people who don't understand the language! I said 'two hours!'" But Escalante was finished.

With an irritated flick of his wrist, the man snatched the test from Escalante's hand and placed it alongside the answer guide. The glower faded slowly from his face as he checked off one correct answer after another. Finally he looked up and said, almost apologetically, "Okay. You did fine. You got every one right."[9]

So by May, when Fabiola and Jaimito arrived in the United States, Jaime was studying English, chemistry, physics, and mathematics at Pasadena City College and working full-time at Van de Kamp's.

At the coffee shop, Escalante worked with a busboy known as Taylor. Taylor was proud of his work record of fifteen years in the same job. He was looking forward to a promotion to dishwasher. He predicted that Escalante would take his place as busboy.

"You know," Escalante responded, "if your objective is to become a dishwasher, you're going to be a dishwasher for another fifteen years. But that's not my goal. I'm going to school and I'm going to get the language. Then I'm going to find a better job. One day I'm going to come back here as a big shot and you'll still be washing dishes."[10]

Mr. Polsky, the manager, encouraged Escalante in his studies. "Jimmy," he called him. "How are you doing?"

"Just fine, sir," Escalante replied in a thick accent.

"Are you learning the language?"

"Yes, sir," he nodded. "I'm in the developing process."

The manager liked Escalante. One day he called him over. "Jimmy," he said, "You look like you're getting the picture of how we do things around here. So I'm going to give you a more attractive job. I'm going to make you a busboy." It was not a great advancement, but it was a little more money and one step up. Not long after that, Polsky handed Escalante a page from a waitress' order pad. "Do you see this paper? You have to be able to understand this writing and read it fast." If he could do that, he could move from busboy to waiter.

Escalante took the ticket home so he could memorize the English words for the restaurant's offerings and learn to decipher the waitresses' scrawls. In a matter of months, his diligence in his job earned him several promotions, finally to head cook. He did not particularly enjoy working in the kitchen, but he liked the increase in pay.

Escalante offered a number of suggestions that impressed his boss. He pointed out that from 6:00 to 7:00 A.M. the coffee shop usually had only one or two customers—and six employees. No one came after noon because the college had its last class at ten and the area had very little traffic when classes were over. So Polsky shortened the shop's hours—and saved money.

Escalante rearranged the dining area, making it more efficient. He expanded the menu, adding new dishes. He cut up the Swiss steaks that were left over from one day and had a tasty, meaty soup the next. When the manager kept ordering bread, he showed him that the freezer was full of loaves and food was being wasted. He calculated the amount of food that was typically consumed and purchased only what was likely to be sold. Polsky was pleased with the dollars Escalante saved him.

"Some day," he promised, "You're going to be in charge of all of this."

But in his heart Escalante said, "You must be dreaming. One day I'm going to leave this job and return to my first love. One day I'll be teaching again."[11]

His advancement at work was steady and rapid, but his progress at the junior college was much slower. While he was studying English, he was also pursuing an Associate of Arts degree. A course in American Institutions was a requirement. In the second week of class, Escalante was relaxing during the break, enjoying a cup of coffee from the lunch truck. His professor called him over.

"Why are you taking this class?" he wanted to know.

"It's a requirement, sir," Escalante replied honestly.

"You know you're not going to make it," the instructor informed him flatly.

Escalante was surprised. "Why, sir?"

The professor listed two reasons. "You don't participate in the class" was the first, and the second was Escalante's accent. "Your accent is very heavy. So I don't think you're going to make it," the instructor repeated. "I would suggest you drop the class."

Stunned, Escalante considered how to respond. Should he return to the class? The professor said that the normal procedure was to talk with a counselor.

As he walked into the counseling office the next day, Escalante wondered what sort of advice the counselor would offer that would help him do well in this difficult class. He explained his situation, recounting the previous night's conversation. The counselor merely asked one question: "Did the professor say you're not going to make it?"

"Yes," Escalante acknowledged. He was expecting a pep talk, a confidence booster, encouragement to persevere. Instead he received what felt like a slap in the face: "If the professor doesn't think you can make it, you probably won't. Just drop the class."

Escalante knew that it was useless to argue or appeal. But he was not going to let this class keep him from obtaining his A.A. degree. He would simply have to take the course in summer school—from a different instructor.

He would never forget the shock of this experience. A professor, whose responsibility should be to motivate as well as educate, and a counselor, whose job was to help students reach their educational goals, were advising a student—a student who wanted to learn—to quit. He would never forget what was for him a contradiction between responsibility and action. But he would not allow this temporary setback to derail his plans for his future. Escalante would not forget this incident, but he would not let it stop him.[12]

DISCIPLINE

 Escalante really wanted to teach. Frying fish and grilling sandwiches could never satisfy him the way a student's thrill of discovery of the laws of physics could. The recognition, promotions, and appreciation from Polsky were nothing compared to the pride of thrusting a hard-earned diploma into the hand of a young person. Even the computer science and other technology he was learning in school, fascinating though it was, could not stimulate his mind and heart like a classroom of teenagers. He wrote to the California Department of Education, sending them copies of his Bolivian credentials and of awards he

had garnered during ten years of teaching as well as a list of the courses he was taking at Pasadena City College. He requested a California teaching credential.

The letter that came in response may as well have been a sledgehammer. An American teaching credential, it explained, required demonstration of competency in American subjects. Basically, he would have to repeat his entire college work—four years of full-time study—plus a fifth year of student teaching.[1]

Escalante's wife was not upset by the news. She had been concerned about the difficulties he would encounter if he taught school in the United States. The system was different from the one in Bolivia. Having girls and boys together in the same classes seemed to invite problems. Also, the students were different: They were less disciplined, less respectful. Her husband had said he was going to start over. This was his chance to pursue the dream of electrical engineering he had abandoned so many years ago.

She did not like to see Escalante working at the coffee shop. He had skills that could command more money and greater prestige. So she began talking to him about another job, a job that could lead to engineering.

Because they needed more income than Van de Kamp's brought in, Fabiola had been working on the assembly line at the Burroughs Corporation's electronics manufacturing plant. (Women were often hired for the painstaking job of wrapping hair-thin wires into coils to produce microvolts for the magnetic heads of computers.)

Fabiola saw in a bulletin that her company was hiring. Jaime, however, was not ready to change. He wanted to finish his education first, and that would take years. He wanted to be more proficient in English. He had not given up his goal of teaching again. Even so, she was able to convince him not only that a job at Burroughs would be better for him, but also that the company needed his skills.[2]

Although his beginning salary at the electronics corporation was less than he had been making at the coffee shop, the job did appear to have some interesting possibilities. Besides, he could continue his classes at night and a five-day work week would give him an extra day to study.

He started out in the parts department. His job was to stock the many components used for assembly and deliver them to the various foremen. Escalante could never be content with such a simple task, so he looked for ways to make it more efficient, more interesting.

He decided to reorganize the storage system. He made boxes and color-coded them. Then he gave the components color codes also. Transistors, capacitors, resistors—all were sorted and placed into boxes that would reveal at a glance exactly what they were and what they could do. This not only impressed his supervisors, but it also reduced his work time. That gave him an opportunity to squeeze in some extra study. Once when he had finished his work, a foreman found Escalante poring over his math book. "Is that color-coded, too?" he chuckled.[3]

A continual problem at Burroughs was the number of computer heads that came off the assembly line unusable. These were the parts of the computer that encode and decode information. Technicians sometimes spent days, even weeks, finding the source of each flaw. The chief technician was very skilled in troubleshooting—discovering the causes of problems and correcting them. He could analyze forty heads a day, pinpointing the "bug" precisely and repairing it perfectly. Unfortunately, he was absent often and the work was not getting done.

On a day when the rejects were piling up and the chief technician was missing, the foreman asked Escalante in exasperation, "How long would it take you to learn how to do this job?"

Escalante did not know. He was not familiar with the way the heads worked. The foreman had an engineer give Escalante a crash course.

"What do you think?" the foreman asked again. "Could you repair them?"

Ever confident, Escalante replied, "I could if you give me blueprints to study."

The foreman hesitated. Burroughs worked with a number of different, competing companies. Blueprints contained closely guarded company secrets. He could not risk those secrets being obtained by a rival, but he had a feeling this parts department clerk could be the answer to his dilemma. So he formulated a plan.

On Friday, the foreman put the blueprints in the trunk of his car. That evening, Escalante parked his little Volkswagen next to the foreman's car and waited until no one was near. Then, with the foreman's extra key, he unlocked the trunk and transferred the charts to his "beetle."

All day Saturday and into the night on Sunday Escalante studied the schematics. The worried foreman called him Sunday evening, checking to see how he was coming along. Escalante told him he had a few questions—some items that were not covered on the blueprints. The foreman promised that he would have someone explain anything he needed. He was mostly concerned that Escalante would be able to return the charts without being seen. "Don't worry about it," Escalante said.

On Monday at 8:00 A.M., the Volkswagen slid into a parking space alongside the foreman's car. The exchange was made quickly and quietly, before anyone else arrived. Escalante kept his questions on separate sheets of paper and the foreman assigned an engineer to answer them.

It took Escalante one or two after-hours sessions of working with the actual heads, matching them to what he learned from the blueprints, before he felt he could analyze and repair most malfunctioning parts. The following Monday the foreman dismissed his chief technician and gave the job to Escalante.

At first, Escalante was slow. Whereas the technician who was fired could diagnose forty heads a day, Escalante did only four or five on his first day in his new position. With each one he got a little better, and after about eight months, Escalante knew magnetic heads inside and out. He had watched their construction at every stage along the assembly line from the very beginning until they were ready to be placed in computers. He had a thorough picture of how and why they worked; he knew them better than the engineers who designed them. His diligence and his careful attention to the tiniest detail earned him a series of promotions, from technician to foreman to tester to senior tester.[4]

No matter how far he advanced, Escalante never forgot anyone he met along the way. One day when he was taking a break, he suggested to the engineer who had joined him that they have coffee at Van de Kamp's. His eyes panned the familiar booths, counters, sinks, and stoves. Sure enough, there was Taylor, still washing dishes.

"Taylor," he called. "Do you remember me?" Taylor remembered.

The engineer was surprised to learn that Escalante had once been a janitor. "I'm just trying to help him out," Escalante explained, referring to Taylor. "I'm trying to stimulate him, motivate him."

It was part teasing, part bragging, that was true. But it was also an attempt to give a man with very shortsighted ambitions a model for success. He wanted Taylor to understand what he would later repeat over and over to every high-school class he taught: Only you can determine what your destiny will be. You need to set a goal for yourself and then go for it! You can accomplish great things if you have dreams, you cultivate the ganas to reach those dreams, and you just keep going.[5]

The discipline Escalante brought to his work resulted in suggestions and innovations that saved Burroughs a considerable amount of money. When Escalante began as a tester, he noticed that there were fourteen employees in the "rework" section. When a head was judged imperfect by quality control, it went to one of the reworkers. If the problem was simple, the employee could locate and fix it in about forty minutes. Escalante asked himself if there could be an easier, more efficient way.

He developed a test device that could detect any common problem with a few flips of switches. Once the malfunction was identified, the reworking was simple. The tester noted the problem—"open," "short circuit," "low impedance," etc.—and sent it to the employee in charge of repairing that particular problem. With the new device and the streamlined procedure, four people could do a better job in less time than fourteen had previously.

Escalante revised the repair card that accompanied faulty heads. Instead of recording in longhand everything that was replaced, employees checked the appropriate codes. This saved several minutes on each operation and minutes could be translated into dollars.

By keeping detailed records, Escalante discovered that in six hours of overtime, with a long break after four, employees could produce as much as they did in eight hours with shorter breaks. He found that using alcohol to clean connectors instead of acetone saved many hours and eliminated certain problems. All his suggestions put more money in the company coffers and smiles on the faces of his supervisors.[6]

A large number of rejects once had Escalante stumped. The foreman was frantic because these heads were part of a large contract the company had with the Federal Bureau of Investigation (FBI). Escalante dissected at least twenty heads, trying to determine the cause of the problem. The same thing was happening in another plant. Finally the foreman decided to send Escalante and two engineers to the main office in Detroit in the hope that experts there could help them figure out what was wrong. The flight was scheduled, the tickets purchased.

Escalante, not willing to accept defeat, kept working, kept eliminating possible solutions, kept narrowing the problem down. Eventually his diligence paid off.

In the playful swagger that was typical Escalante style, he baited the foreman before revealing his findings. "I'm sorry, sir," he announced somewhat dramatically on the morning of the flight. "I'm not going to Detroit."

The foreman bit. "Why are you saying this?" he panicked. It was an important project. The plane was to leave at 2:00 that afternoon.

"I'm not going, sir," Escalante insisted, his eyes twinkling. The foreman was not certain whether Escalante was serious or teasing. He tried to reason with him. He pointed out his responsibility to the company. He reminded him that Burroughs was paying for Escalante to take math and electronics classes at the University of Southern California.

"Yes, sir. I understand that, sir. I'm not going because I know what the problem is."

The somewhat relieved foreman wondered how Escalante had solved a puzzle that had mystified so many engineers. Escalante played the game a little longer. "Was it in the gap line?" the foreman guessed.

Even though he was successful at Burroughs, Escalante still longed to begin teaching again. The hat he is wearing in this photo is now called an "Escalante hat" in Bolivia.

"No, sir."

"Was it impedance?"

"No, sir." The problem was almost humorously simple. Each completed head was stamped with a seven-digit number. Escalante had discovered that the chemicals in the ink used to stamp them contained metal—a minuscule amount of metal, but enough to create a short circuit in the delicate head. When the ink was cleaned from the heads, they worked perfectly.

The foreman refused to trust anyone but Escalante to repair the defective parts. So Escalante worked about forty hours overtime and the FBI had its materials on schedule. Then Burroughs changed its ink.[7]

Escalante contributed much to the Burroughs Corporation. His timesaving suggestions, cost-cutting ideas, and other innovations increased the company's profitability. The people at Burroughs were good to Escalante also. They bestowed awards and other forms of recognition. They paid his night-school tuition. They sent him to Guadalajara, Mexico, to teach engineering seminars and to Europe and other places to make technical presentations.

After about five years, the work at Burroughs had ceased to excite him. At first, he had enjoyed uncovering problems and finding solutions. Then so much of the job had become routine: the same equipment, the same components, the same procedures. He found himself dealing not with people but with computers and blueprints and papers. Even during breaks, conversations with coworkers centered on computers, diagrams, and electronic parts. He missed the stimulation of creative human interaction. He longed for the challenge of young minds that could be awakened to the fascinations of the world around them and the world of fascinations within them.[8]

For the entire eight years he was at Burroughs and the years at Van de Kamp's before, he had continued to attend school, working steadily toward a degree in math. In his final semester before graduation from California State University, Los Angeles, in 1973, one of his instructors cornered him. The professor had come to admire his knowledge and skills in electronics.

"Jaime," he asked, "what are you going to do with your math degree?"

Without a moment's hesitation he answered, "I'm going to teach."

The professor was surprised that such an intelligent, talented, and gifted electronics wizard would choose to work with teenagers. But Escalante had taught in Bolivia for ten years and had not grown tired of the ever-new parade of students with all their youthful exuberance, their self-doubts, their laughter and tears, and their limitless potential.

"If you really want to teach," the professor offered, "there is a way you could be in the classroom in a year."[9]

HARD WORK

The winner of the National Science Foundation scholarship could indeed teach in just one year. The award covered tuition and books and even provided a $150-per-week stipend for living expenses. The recipient would study full-time at the University of Southern California; California State, Los Angeles; and California State, Fullerton. Listing the intensive program on a job application guaranteed a good shot at a teaching position.

Escalante was eager to fill out the application, but his wife was not pleased. She was afraid that undisciplined American students would frustrate her husband. Besides, they had a second son now—Fernando was four years old—and a teacher's salary would be lower than Escalante's wages as a senior tester. She was proud of his accomplishments at Burroughs and wished the complexities of the electronics industry and his many successes in it would be enough to satisfy his need to be doing, to be challenged, to be contributing.

But Escalante's dream was to teach again and the scholarship would mean he could reach his dream sooner. "I'm going to do this," he declared softly. She knew he had to. Inwardly she hoped he would not win the scholarship, but she did not try to dissuade him again.[1]

He impressed the scholarship committee with some number tricks, some creative lesson plans, and some unconventional ways of handling students.[2] Committee members were less concerned with his age (forty-two) and his heavy accent than with his knowledge of math and his ability to communicate that knowledge to others. They gave him the scholarship.

One year later, in 1974, just as his professor had promised, Escalante was ready for the classroom. With a California teaching credential, which he had worked toward for ten years, finally in his possession, Escalante was sitting in the personnel office of the Los Angeles Unified School District. The placement director asked him where he wanted to work.

Escalante was confused. In Bolivia, the Department of Education told teachers where they were to be. He was not sure what the interviewer was asking. Where did he want to work?

"A school, sir," he answered as plainly as he knew how. When the director realized that Escalante did not understand the question or the procedure, he opened a map and described various parts of the city to him. He showed him sections that were primarily Anglo, neighborhoods that were mostly African-American, large Mexican-American areas, and pockets of Asian-Americans. Then he asked him again where he wanted to teach.

It seemed only natural that a Spanish-speaking immigrant teach Mexican-American children. Besides, the barrios were not far from where he lived. The district gave him the names of the principals of three schools in East L.A.[3]

He did not choose Garfield High over the others; it was simply the first school on the list. When the principal noticed the experience with computers on his resume and offered him a position as a computer teacher, Escalante did not want to look any further. This was perfect! He knew computers backwards and forwards and he understood practical applications from industry. He had all kinds of equipment he could use to captivate students and prepare them for modern careers. Escalante could hardly wait for September.

He began his new job the day before the students were scheduled to arrive. Escalante had been called to his first teachers' meeting. When he examined the class schedule he had been given, he was puzzled. What was high-school math, he wondered. He understood the words algebra, geometry, trigonometry— but high-school math? And where were the computer classes he had spent the summer designing?

He was not prepared for the explanation. The computer classes were the wishful thinking of the principal; the school had no money for additional computers or computer teachers. High-school math meant basic mathematical functions: multiplication, division, fractions, and percents. Escalante had five periods of what he considered "Mickey Mouse things."[4]

The textbooks were another surprise. It was bad enough that he would need to figure out how to create some enthusiasm for very simple concepts, but, according to the curriculum, high-school math was even more basic than the name implied. He would have thought every fifth grader had mastered the principles in the textbooks he was given.

The first day of classes might have utterly discouraged a less determined newcomer. The grounds were littered with bits of paper. The entire campus was spattered with graffiti. The territorial markings were everywhere: on building walls, on desks, in textbooks, even in some teachers' roll books. A guard patrolled the grounds and the parking lots.

Many of the students were just as Fabiola had said they would be. They displayed little respect in their actions, their clothing, or their language. They sauntered into class late, without paper, pencils, or books. They brought their own reading material and shared it with their friends while teachers lectured. They wore gang colors or provocative blouses that drew attention away from blackboards. Their speech was peppered with profanities.

Their performance was pathetic. Some were recent immigrants and had difficulty speaking English. Several simply did not turn in homework. Many counted on their fingers.[5]

This was going to take work, Escalante realized—hard work. But hard work was second nature to him. He had spent ten years getting to this point, and he was not about to give up now. His specialty was starting from zero and building something good. He had done it as a young boy with neighbors' castoffs. He had done it at Villarroel. He had done it when he came to the United States. And he would do it with these students.

Their performance was low, he reasoned, not because they came from disadvantaged neighborhoods, but because no one expected much from them. Why else was he teaching five periods of high-school math?

Escalante would begin by creating an environment that pointed them toward achievement. When he finally got his own classroom, he enlisted students' help in brightening it. Together they scraped old color from the walls and fresh graffiti from the desks. They painted the room a clean, inviting white.[6] Then they hung colorful posters of people who had dreamed big and made their dreams come true: Joe Montana, quarterback for the San Francisco Forty-Niners; Wayne Gretzky with his hockey stick; Bobby Bonilla, then with the Pittsburg Pirates; and Michael Jordan, stuffing a two-pointer into the basket. Escalante loved sports and thought the images of these superstar athletes would remind his students that ordinary people can reach lofty goals.

If pictures of heroes were not enough to encourage these children of the barrio to dream, Escalante interspersed them with other inspirational posters. From any place they sat in his room, students could read "Mission Possible," "What I See in My Mind Is What I Get in My Life," and "I'll Be a Success."

He knew, too, that high expectations alone would not turn these kids around. They needed discipline also. So, he refused admittance to tardy students. He ejected unruly ones. He sent students to the principal's office for small infractions. When he distributed textbooks, he made students sign for them, warning them that they would be charged twenty-five dollars if

Escalante began teaching at Garfield using a combination of discipline, motivation, and creative teaching techniques.

a book was damaged.[7] He had a form, in English and Spanish, to be signed by uncooperative students that said: "I do not want to do my classwork nor my homework. I do not want to follow the teacher's instructions. I am very happy with a grade of FAIL."

He secured the aid of parents. At the beginning of a school term, he called each home. Often he asked each mother to tell her child she did not want to hear from the teacher again. This gave the threat of a phone call later in the year greater force. He was known to call at five in the morning in order to catch a father at home.[8] On more than one occasion he phoned or visited parents he thought were holding back their youths' progress.

The stringent discipline and heavy demands in Escalante's classroom were tempered with quick humor and affectionate banter. If students' attention wandered, they were told to get a shoeshine kit or enroll in cosmetology classes.[9] If a boy's hair was too long for his teacher's tastes, Escalante threatened to pull it out. Students who could not answer questions correctly were seated near the door so they could be expelled from class quickly. A girl wearing heavy makeup was asked if she had a contract with Dracula.[10]

Not everyone appreciated the teacher's pricks and prods. Sometimes there were angry comebacks, frustrated outbursts, and threats to drop his class. If he provoked anger rather than compliance, he felt that he had succeeded at least in awakening some energy he could channel to the student's profit.

Because he could not remember names, and to bestow a sense of specialness on each student, Escalante coined nicknames for them: "Lieutenant" for someone who walked straight and stiff, "Fingerman" for a boy who counted on his fingers, "Elizabeth Taylor" or "Sophia Loren" for an attractive girl. They, in turn, gave him the name "Kemo" after the Lone Ranger's title "Kemo Sabe."[11] It meant "wise one."

If Escalante could not recall a student's name or the nickname he had assigned, he simply called him "Johnny."

The problem Escalante had remembering names caused at least one misunderstanding. Two boys in the same class had the same name; one was a bright, attentive student and the other was, in Escalante's estimation, lazy. One mother asked Escalante how her son was doing. Assuming her boy was the cooperative Johnny, he praised him, assuring his mother he was happy to have him in his class. The next day, the lazy Johnny beamed, and from that moment on, he did his assignments eagerly and well. "I didn't know," he told his teacher, "that anybody wanted me in his class."[12]

Escalante's difficulty with names did not mean he did not know his students. He knew all about them. He knew which ones were in band or cheerleading or sports. He knew who had jobs and where they worked. He knew from the beginning which ones were quick and which ones needed extra help, which ones were motivated and which ones were lazy.

He worked hard at finding ways to help his students understand the language of math. He often turned math problems into ridiculous questions that caught and held the attention of his students: "If Juan has five times as many girlfriends as Pedro . . . "[13] He framed the unfamiliar terminology in the contexts of sports and other everyday activities. Division by zero, for example, which is impossible, he called "illegal defense."[14] The minus sign in front of a set of parentheses, which changes all pluses inside the parentheses to minuses and all minuses to pluses, became the "secret agent." "Marching band" meant that the solution could be found very simply, by following normal procedures step by step.[15]

Once he found the various sparks that ignited the ganas within each student, he worked hard to keep their motivation strong. He began each class with a quiz and gave tests weekly so they remained alert. He adjusted the clock on his wall frequently, sometimes setting it ahead and sometimes behind, so no one but he knew the correct time.[16] If a student's attention was lagging, he pounded him or her playfully with a small pillow, kept just for that purpose. It was not done in anger or even in frustration, but firmly and affectionately.[17]

Everything about him—his exaggerated facial expressions, his classroom theatrics, his sarcastic barbs—everything was calculated to push his students to the peak of performance. Even Escalante's clothes figured in his teaching methodology. A casual observer might think he wore the same slacks and shirt each day. The monotonous sameness removed one potential source of distraction.[18]

In the midst of the motivational toys, the basketball metaphors, the blackboard examples, the drills, and the tests, Escalante lectured his classes about their lives and their enormous potential. "You do not enter the future," he would tell them. "You make the future. So set your goals and keep working. Keep going."[19] He reminded them that knowledge is power, and he wanted them to grab all the power they could.

"You have to respect yourself," he admonished.[20]

He lectured to inspire determination. He described Babe Ruth's famous home run, before which the baseball player pointed toward the spot where he intended the ball to go. He quoted the famous athlete as saying, "It never entered my mind to do anything *but* hit a home run."[21]

"You can become whatever you want to be," he reminded them constantly.[22]

He lectured to encourage discipline. He talked about Jerry West, the Los Angeles Lakers basketball player dubbed "Mr. Clutch" by the sportscasters because he usually came through in tight spots. "I call him 'Mr. Consistency,'" Escalante said, "because every day he shoots baskets at least 500 times."[23]

"You can do it if you make yourselves work at it" was the understood message.

He lectured on the importance of hard work. "An employer will not want to hear your problems," he predicted. An employer would care only how hard they were willing to work.[24]

He wanted them to believe they could accomplish great things and to have the personal qualities they would need to reach their goals. "You can do it," he insisted. "You are the true dreamers."

If someone seemed to miss the points of the general class lectures, he would provide a private session. Sometimes he whispered to young students who were struggling with low self-image, "You're gifted." He reinforced his statement by declaring that the student had an IQ of 230. When students protested that IQs could not go that high, Escalante assured them he had the true formula for measuring intelligence and, by that formula, they were gifted.[25]

Once he complimented a girl on the new sweater she was wearing. He feigned surprise that she had picked out something with colors that were so flattering. He said he wanted to bring his camera and take a picture. "You must be gifted," he told her.

A week later the girl approached him with growing confidence. "Kemo, are you going to bring your camera tomorrow? I'm going to wear my sweater."[26]

The students were not always sure what was fact and what was part of the game he played to provoke them to excellence. But they knew he cared about them and they sensed he was probably right. He was making progress with them.

But the progress was slow—and not nearly enough. He wanted to take them beyond the basics of learning math and graduating from high school. He wanted to expand their abilities and their horizons, to convince them that they could do anything. He wanted to see them set their sights on a lofty goal and give it everything they had. He longed to have them savor the sweet taste of success.

SUCCESS

In his second year at Garfield, the school had a new principal and Escalante had persuaded him to add some algebra courses to his teaching load. That year and the next two, he was able to take his students a little farther in math, but he knew they were capable of more. They just needed a challenge.

In 1978, Escalante found the ideal vehicle: the Advanced Placement (A.P.) calculus exam. The A.P. exam was a test of college-level math skills that was taken by only 3 percent of seniors preparing to enter college.[1] It could earn a student up to five units of college credit for a course taken in high school. Even more, it would push his students to obtain the skills they needed for high-paying jobs. It would force them to learn analytical and problem-solving techniques they could apply in any profession. It was an objective measure, testing what students knew against a nationwide standard rather than against a teacher's norms. It would give them a head start in college and in life.

The objectivity of the exam made it a challenge for the teacher as well as the students. They would form a team, with Escalante as the coach, and together they would train and drill and fight to beat the test.

Preparation for such a venture should be a four-year process. Before a student could take calculus, he or she would have to have mastered algebra 2, trigonometry, and mathematical analysis. Los Angeles high schools in the 1970s and 1980s, however, were three-year institutions, and with twenty-five classes of high-school math being taught,[2] few students had the academic background for a college-level class. Still, it was a wonderful goal. If he started now, encouraging his best students to attempt the test, perhaps in three or four years he could have entire classes ready for the challenge.

As he prepared for his first A.P. calculus class, Escalante wondered how he could, in one school year, teach not only calculus but also the missing prerequisites. His first thought was to require the A.P.

students to take trig and math analysis in the summer before school resumed.

It was not easy, but he talked the principal into allowing him to teach a summer school course that would lay the foundation for calculus. Unfortunately, a severe and sudden financial crisis in the state of California forced cutbacks for every government agency, including school districts. Escalante's summer math class was cancelled before it even began.

If the high school could not help, perhaps a local college might. Colleges should welcome the opportunity to assist disadvantaged youth who might eventually become their students, he reasoned. But the two universities and one community college he approached had also been caught in the state budget squeeze. They could offer no help.

His only solution was to require extra time of his A.P. students. They would have to begin before school opened each day, stay after their friends went home, and come back on Saturdays.

He began the class in 1978 with fourteen students, chosen from those who had previous exposure to math analysis. He let them know from the beginning about the rigorous demands of a college-level class. Within two weeks, seven students had dropped the class. Another two followed shortly thereafter.[3]

Escalante was disappointed that only three girls and two boys had the ganas to stretch beyond what was comfortable, but he was determined to work hard with these five. He felt like a curve was thrown to him a month before the exam when he learned that the test required an administration fee for each student. Undaunted, he organized car washes and sales of candied apples to raise the money.[4] Hadn't he told them ganas would overcome any obstacle?

They took the exam in May, 1979. A score of three or above was considered passing and earned the student college credit. Four of the five passed.

An eighty percent success rate was wonderful, especially for the first time anyone passed an A.P. calculus test in the school's history[5] and considering all the hurdles this class had to face. But Escalante was not satisfied. He was determined to include more students the following year. He enlisted the help of another teacher in beefing up some of the prerequisite classes. He coaxed particularly promising students into his program. That year (1979–1980) eight of the ten calculus students passed the exam, twice the number of the preceding year.

To underscore the level of commitment needed for his courses, Escalante devised a contract for his next year's classes between himself, his students, and their parents. The students agreed to be in class; to do the assigned homework; to attend special, one-and-a-half-hour-long after-school classes four days a week; and to cooperate fully in all their classes. Parents agreed to help and encourage their children to do as they promised. Escalante agreed to teach them everything they needed. In that year, fourteen of fifteen students—ninety-three percent—passed the Advanced Placement test.

Escalante's success at motivating young people, maintaining good discipline, and facilitating achievement won him the recognition of the other math teachers—recognition that was both positive and negative. Some of the teachers admired him greatly. A few became disciples, asking him for suggestions and using some of his methodologies. Others were annoyed at what they perceived to be his arrogance. They saw his passion for pushing kids to their limit as a criticism of their own teaching abilities. They felt his zeal for higher mathematics ignored the great majority of the student body. They thought he was too hard on students.

Despite the controversy surrounding his work and his style, his peers elected him chairman of the math department in 1981. It was an honor, but he considered its responsibilities a nuisance that kept him from his students. He had little tolerance for meetings, which he believed were a waste of time, so he simply did not attend meetings of department leaders and did not schedule many meetings of the math department. This further irritated a number of his colleagues, who felt that he was not fulfilling the responsibilities of his position.[6]

Escalante ignored both some of the duties of department chair and the mounting criticism of his fellow teachers. He had eighteen students enrolled in his Advanced Placement calculus class, the largest group yet. He had work to do.

The atmosphere in Escalante's room was much like that in the locker room at a football game. Class began with warm-up exercises. All the students slapped their hands against their desks and stomped their feet on the floor in rhythm while chanting an opening ritual. When attention dropped, Escalante would begin the "wave," a cheer in which row after row of students, in succession, stood, raising their hands, then sat quickly, creating a ripple across the room like a pennant billowing in victory. The intensity of drills and quizzes was relieved with jokes, demonstrations, and an occasional round of volleyball.[7] Just as the classroom clock never registered the correct time, the routine usually varied, keeping the team alert and focused.

Escalante's lectures were seldom boring. Aside from his entertaining, fast-paced style, he could explain very complex mathematical operations with metaphors that were both simple to comprehend and difficult to forget. For example, he taught the concept of absolute value, crucial to the mastery of calculus, in terms of the three-second violation in basketball.[8] He explained graphing functions and limits through illustrations of baseball pitchers and catchers with fastballs and knuckleballs.[9]

Escalante used analogies to clue his students as to how to proceed in solving problems. If he said, "Green light," they knew they could begin with some basic, routine steps. "Red light" meant they should stop and study the problem again. When he called out, "Face mask!" they looked for a mistake they had made at the start of the attempted solution, just as a football player would be assessed a penalty for tugging at a player's face mask near the start of a play.[10]

Everything Escalante did—making up code words for mathematical procedures; giving pet names to his students; and holding after-school, lunchtime, and vacation study sessions—everything was engineered to build a unified team. His calculus students had a language of their own, a camaraderie among themselves, and a coach who knew their every strength and weakness. The 1981–1982 class was a strong, disciplined team.

The big game of that class, the Advanced Placement test, was only two months away. Ordinarily, the thought of how much more his team needed to know and the thrill of watching them absorb it was enough to keep their teacher darting from one activity to the next. This day, however, was different.

His family noticed it. Escalante's twenty-six-year-old son, Jaime Escalante, Jr., had heard his father's restlessness several times in the night and guessed from his subdued manner that he was not feeling well. His father denied any problem, attributing his lethargic mood to disagreements with other math teachers.

His students noticed it. They were surprised to see him sit rather than dance all over the room. Today was the first day they had ever seen his classroom door closed at lunchtime. They asked him if he felt well. One told him he looked a little yellow.[11]

By late morning Escalante admitted to himself that the pain in his side was severe. He had been told before that he had gallstones. He had shrugged it off then and he resolved to do the same now. Escalante gritted his teeth and drove stoically to the class he conducted at night. Even though he enjoyed working at Garfield, and even with the before-school and after-school "intensive-care" study times for his students, he still had empty hours and more to give. So he taught a course in basic math for adults, most of whom were learning to speak English.

Halfway through the class, a sharp pain wrenched his side. He thought a drink of water might help, so he left the room and began to walk down the stairs to the fountain on the floor below. His legs buckled, his hands weakened, and his vision blurred. Five minutes later he awoke at the bottom of the steps with a gash above his eye and blood dried on his face.

At the hospital, the doctor told him he had suffered a mild heart attack. Jaime did not want to believe the diagnosis and he did not have the time to follow the doctor's orders: at least two weeks' rest at home. Fabiola came to take him home from the hospital sooner than the doctor wished. Jaime's heart may have been weakened, but his spirit was still feisty. As his wife stepped from the vehicle, Jaime, with a bandage still covering the cut above his eye, slid behind the steering wheel and pointed the car toward school.[12]

The incident had two effects on his students. First, it bolstered their resolve to do well in his class. They reasoned that if teaching them was this important to him, then they needed to work their hardest to learn, to show him their appreciation.[13] Second, it left a small gap in their ability to solve calculus problems.[14] For a few days, substitute teachers had tried their best to fill that gap.

May 19 was the day for which the calculus team had trained for three years. They were nervous but confident. Escalante had frequently told them they were the best, and today they were determined to prove that statement true. The eighteen students were seated at desks spread out across the room, given their test booklets, and monitored carefully as they dug into the problems. In a few hours they were finished.

It was two months before the results were reported. Escalante was not worried about the test

E scalante's entire 1982 A.P. calculus class passed the Advanced Placement calculus exam.

scores. His students had been well prepared and he was certain most of them would pass.

He was, however, elated when the Garfield counselor called. All eighteen students had scored three or above! The team had a one hundred percent pass rate![15]

PLAYING
DEFENSE

 Escalante had always warned his students that they had to play defense. He had advised them to anticipate problems and have alternate plans in mind, for problems would surely come. He had taught them to live offensively—to set goals and to go after them wholeheartedly. He had also cautioned that, even for the most determined, life was seldom smooth. They should always be ready with a good defense. "You are winners," he told them over and over again. "But don't get too comfortable."

"Even after you've given your total commitment," he had often said, "and you have finally reached your goal and you see the light at the end of the tunnel—watch out. It will be an incoming train."

He had told them. He had written it on the board. He had given them examples. Still, neither he nor his students were prepared for the defensive move that was required by the events of the summer of 1982.[1]

The vacation period began happily enough. Unable to spend any extended period of time simply relaxing, Escalante was teaching in the Upward Bound program at Occidental College, giving disadvantaged high-school students the extra help they needed to be ready for college. At the same time, he was negotiating to put together a summer course to give Garfield students a more solid foundation in higher math. He had plans to visit his family in Bolivia toward the end of summer, and on weekends he was enjoying his swimming pool. Several of his students had been accepted at very good colleges: University of California, Los Angeles (UCLA); University of California, Berkeley; California Polytechnic State University; California State University; Columbia; Princeton; Harvard. It promised to be a good summer.

The first hint of trouble came in a phone call to Escalante's home from a student who had scored a four on the A.P. calculus exam two months earlier.

"Kemo, I am so mad!" she sputtered.

He could not guess what could have upset this fiery, determined girl. He had thought she was enrolled at UCLA and beginning an orientation program. He had assumed she was doing well. But now she was barely able to control her voice. She had received a letter from the Educational Testing Service that accused her of cheating on the A.P. exam and cancelled her grade. Escalante was as puzzled as she was angry.

One by one, other students reported that they had received similar letters. A girl who was enrolled at Princeton had just returned home from a summer premedical program and opened her mail. First she saw her score of five. Then she read the letter. Another had to fly home from her yearly visit to her grandparents in Guadalajara, Mexico, after her father and mother opened the letter. A boy who had dreamed and worked hard toward a career in medical research received his letter after a week-long vacation in Mazatlán, Mexico. The class valedictorian read her letter through angry tears. She had counted on the three Advanced Placement tests she had taken to shave a semester off her college program.

In all, of the eighteen students on the calculus team, fourteen were suspected of copying answers. Their scores were all declared invalid.

Escalante tried to ease his students' rage and confusion. "I'll call the principal, I'll find out," he assured them. "Don't worry about it."[2]

When he phoned the Educational Testing Service (E.T.S.), which administered the exam, no one would talk with him. The officials said that privacy rights required that they deal with the students individually and directly. They refused to discuss the situation with anyone but the students themselves.

What they did not tell Escalante was that a single question on the test had been difficult for all his students. They had breezed through the forty-five multiple-choice questions with little hesitation. The seven word problems—free response questions— were considerably harder, but Escalante's drills and basketball imagery had leapt to their minds and they had plodded methodically through the solutions. Question number six, however, had stumped them. The formulas for volume, area, and cost that it required had been taught by a substitute while Escalante was in the hospital. Many of the students could not think of the correct formula. They began with similar, inaccurate equations and the E.T.S. concluded that they had somehow copied from one another.[3]

The letter from the E.T.S. gave the students three options for clearing up the problem. They could (a) admit to the cheating, (b) provide evidence that the grades were valid, or (c) retake the test.[4] Whatever they chose, they had to act before school resumed in September or they could not receive the college credit their grades had earned them.

Admission of wrongdoing that did not occur seemed absurd to them. Proving that they had not copied appeared impossible. Taking the exam again after two months without any studying seemed equally ridiculous.

Two of the students who received the letters did not want to take any action. One had already started at Columbia University, working toward a degree in medicine, and could not spare the time to contest math credits. Another was serving in the army.[5]

Of the remaining twelve, some tried the second option. They had some of their teachers write character references. One argued that his high grade point average indicated he would have had no need to cheat. They described Escalante's practice of using drills and other forms of repetition and tried to show how reasonable it was that all his students would solve problems the same way. None of their arguments impressed the E.T.S.

The testing service sent two officials to Garfield to learn what they could of the circumstances under which the test had been given. They examined the room where the students had sat, they saw the unlocked cabinet where the exams had been stored, and they questioned the counselor who had administered the test. They learned nothing that would change their minds.[6]

Escalante could not understand why the E.T.S. was so insistent that his students had cheated—and so unwilling to talk with him. He wondered if it was because the students were all Hispanic.

As the standoff dragged on, the principal made arrangements to visit the E.T.S. regional office to see what he could discover about what had aroused suspicion in the first place. He invited Escalante to meet him there. Since the principal was late, Escalante went into the office alone.

The E.T.S. official tried to explain the scoring procedures, but he refused to show the actual exams to Escalante. That would violate the students' privacy, he said.

Escalante exploded in anger. He suggested to the official, who was himself Hispanic, that the E.T.S. was discriminating against Latino students. He refused to believe the testing service had any foundation for its accusations. "You're chasing a black cat in a dark room," he spat as he stormed out.[7]

As the last days of summer ticked by, option two had all but disintegrated. The principal, the proctor who had supervised the test, and several teachers had sent impassioned letters to the E.T.S. Students had mailed their notebooks. Escalante, responding to an E.T.S. request, had solved three of the problems on the test and submitted his work, but the students could not convince the testing service that their scores were honestly obtained. Their only choices were to forget the whole thing or to take the test over.

A letter from E.T.S. pressed the decision. Dated August 24, 1982, it informed the students that a retest had been scheduled for August 31. They had three days to make arrangements to test on that day and that day only or the grades from their exams would be cancelled.

Angrily the students and their teacher discussed the pros and cons. Some thought taking the test over would be an admission of guilt. Some did not care if they got the college credit. All felt that a few days was not nearly enough time to review so much material, especially since no one had looked at any of it in three months.

In the end, it was their respect for Escalante more than their desire to be vindicated that made the decision. They wanted to show him that they remembered what he had taught, that they appreciated all the time he had poured into preparing them, and that they were everything he said they were. "We ought to do it for him," they agreed. "He deserves it."[8] So they arranged to meet together one more time.

The next Saturday morning was like old times. The coach opened the gates at 7:00 A.M. The team assembled in their old room. They studied and drilled and practiced. They reviewed basics. They remembered formulas. They solved a host of problems. Then they munched on hamburgers and french fries and talked about their summer. After lunch, Escalante was ready to resume training, but they were finished. They had played defense for two months. Tuesday would be the final game.

The E.T.S. made sure there would be no questioning the results of this exam. They sent two of their own officials to monitor the test. They seated the students as far from one another as physically possible. They watched them carefully. About four hours later it was over.

All morning long Escalante paced aimlessly through his house. He was at home, but his mind and his heart were at Garfield. His wife tried to get him to mow the lawn or watch television—anything to calm his nerves. He was waiting for news from his players.

At 12:30 the same student who had been the first to tell him about the E.T.S. letter called to report for the team. "Kemo, it was *hard*," she moaned.

"Don't worry about it," he said. "The game's over."[9]

After two weeks, the E.T.S. had scored the second set of tests. Garfield's principal sat in his office with Escalante at his side, the telephone to his ear, and a pencil poised to record the results.

"Four," he repeated the number given him from the other end of the line. "Three. Five. Five." By the time he reached the last name on the list, he had written four threes, three fours, and five fives. All had passed—again.

The principal was ecstatic over the scores; Escalante was delighted with what they meant. Honor had been restored to his students. They had proven that they had deserved their original scores. They had beaten not only a test, but also a faceless bureaucracy that had falsely accused them. They had learned not only mathematical principles, but the life skills their teacher had sought to develop in them. They had not given up. They had demonstrated the ganas to play defense and they had won. Through determination, discipline, and hard work, they had succeeded—twice.

AFTERMATH OF SUCCESS

In a matter of months, Garfield's amazing accomplishment was heralded in local, state, and national newspapers. It was even broadcast as far away as La Paz, where Jaime's sister Olimpia heard the report on her radio. She wept joyful tears, thrilled that her brother in America was doing so well.[1]

The entire math department was affected by their chairman's achievement. Several teachers who wanted to learn how to motivate students to perform to their full capabilities began to observe him in his classroom and to incorporate some of his techniques in their teaching. In his position as department chairman, Escalante took advantage of the spotlight on higher math to immediately cut the number of basic math classes in half and to reduce it still further—to nine—in the following year, 1984.[2]

The favorable publicity generated positive changes throughout the school. By 1987, 15 percent of the entire student body was enrolled in calculus classes.[3] Advanced Placement programs in other subjects, such as English, history, and science, began to gain in

Escalante (center) led training programs for math teachers. Here he poses with teachers from Los Angeles schools.

popularity. Their successes were creating an atmosphere in which attendance and homework became positive values in the classroom and students aimed for higher goals. The principal noted that the creation of "new role models" was reducing the incidence of vandalism, graffiti, drug use, and gang involvement.[4]

Educators around the country profited from Escalante's acclaim. He was invited to speak at conferences and to teach seminars. He appeared on a Public Broadcasting Corporation television special and developed a TV teaching series called "Futures," which won more than twenty awards.[5] He was congratulated personally by the president of the United States, Ronald Reagan, and later by his successor, George Bush. He served on a White House advisory committee.

One of the ironies for Escalante was that among all the successes and publicity and praise, he remembered those who, in his own pursuit of education, had tried to discourage rather than encourage him to reach his dream. He recalled the man who did not want to give a college entrance exam to an applicant who struggled with the English language. He thought of the professor who had bluntly predicted, "You're not going to make it." He remembered the counselor whose only advice had been, "Drop the class."

Feeling a little mischievous one day, Escalante went to the phone and called the college professor. He

J aime Escalante dines with President Ronald Reagan at the
White House.

found out when his office hours were and arranged to
meet him. When he walked into the office, the
instructor greeted him blankly.

"You should remember me," Escalante prodded.
"My name is Jaime Escalante." The professor did not
remember.

"It was several years ago," Escalante explained. "I
was grabbing a cup of coffee next to the chemistry
building and you suggested I drop your class. You told

me I was not going to make it. Now do you remember?" The professor still could not recall.

"You know what?" Escalante said. "I came to the conclusion, sir, that you are the one who did not make it. I made it," he proclaimed emphatically, waving a 1983 *Reader's Digest* before the astonished professor's face. The magazine had a four-page article trumpeting the teacher's accomplishments. "I made it into the *Reader's Digest*," he pointed out, "and you didn't! Have a good day, sir."[6]

The saying "Success breeds success" is true. Escalante was able to use the publicity and the admiration to develop an increasingly better math department for an increasingly larger group of students. Support for his program was much easier to come by now that its effectiveness had been so clearly demonstrated. Garfield's principal offered him all the tools he asked for: additional books, a teaching assistant, and a larger room. A number of corporations and foundations began to contribute to the school on his behalf, to the tune of about seven hundred fifty thousand dollars each year.[7] East Los Angeles College found a way to fund summer and Saturday math programs for his students. For four years Escalante had lobbied unsuccessfully for some way to teach the calculus prerequisites in intensive summer courses.

The summer program was a special challenge. He needed more than an entertaining style to lure

In 1991, almost five hundred students enrolled in the summer program that prepared them for taking A.P. Calculus at Garfield High School. Their shirts say "Ganas."

teenagers away from television reruns, souped-up cars, and lazy friends. So he created incentives. He obtained tickets from movie theaters, promising the managers their donations would be recognized in the newspapers. He went to food vendors, asking if they would contribute what they had left at the end of the day, and to markets, requesting apples, bread, or anything else that looked good to him. Then he fed his students healthy lunches and gave them free movie tickets.[8]

He continued to pursue his primary work and his real love: teaching. He assigned himself five different classes so each hour would bring a fresh challenge. He increased the team spirit in his A.P. classes by outfitting the students with team jackets and sweatshirts. Even when a benefactor supplied all the funds for testing fees, he helped his students raise money by washing cars so they could take pride in helping themselves. He taught four classes in night school.[9]

Successes built upon successes. The achievement of the class of 1982 was not a rare phenomenon—as Escalante would say, a "one-shot deal." Each year afterwards, the math department became stronger. More and more students passed the A.P. calculus exam: 31 (1983), 63 (1984), 77 (1985), 78 (1986), 87 (1987).[10]

Only a handful of schools across the country did as well, and none had the low-income students Garfield did.

By this time, 1987, Hollywood was attracted to this unusual story. When film producer Tom Musca and director Ramon Menendez first came to Garfield with an idea for a movie that would tell the story of the class that passed the A.P. calculus exam two times, Escalante was reluctant to take a large chunk of his time and attention away from his growing number of students. "Go ahead and write [the screenplay]," he conceded, "but I really don't have much time to deal with you."[11]

The filmmakers, however, coaxed Escalante into assisting them with the story line and other aspects of production. They cast Edward James Olmos as Escalante. The actor had grown up in the East L.A. neighborhoods where the movie was set. Escalante

Escalante (right) poses with actor and friend, Edward James Olmos. Olmos portrayed Escalante in *Stand and Deliver.*

agreed to allow Olmos to shadow him for eighteen hours a day for a full month so he could recreate the teacher's mannerisms, his speech, and his facial expressions. Olmos had his hair thinned so he would look more like Escalante.[12]

The actor and his subject became friends,[13] teaming up to push the moviemakers back into the real-life story whenever their creativity sought to change it. Together Olmos and Escalante persuaded the director and the producer to have the cast meet the students they were playing—and they talked the writers into adjusting the screenplay to keep it more in line with the facts. This insistence on realism led to some stormy production meetings[14] but it resulted in a movie Escalante called "ninety percent factual."[15]

Escalante was also pleased with Olmos's portrayal of him. As he watched the progress of filming for the movie *Stand and Deliver*, he expected to see an actor playing a part. Instead he saw a man he called "100 percent Escalante."[16]

The good performance of the 1982 class was not a fleeting thing. The students had experienced firsthand what determination, discipline, and hard work could accomplish. They believed their teacher when he told them they could achieve anything. They dared to dream big dreams for themselves and to pursue them. Most of them went to college. They earned degrees in psychology, microbiology, anthropology, business, computer science, and aerospace engineering. They became accountants, architects, auditors, medical technicians, engineers, and teachers.[17]

Garfield's math students joined the parade of people showering attention on their hard but caring taskmaster. Three former students approached him on campus after lunch one day.

"Kemo!" they called. "Congratulations!"

Escalante smiled his thanks as he strove to recall these three Johnnys. They were not in any of his calculus classes. They reminded him that he had taught them high-school math some years earlier. Now they were employed in an auto body shop.

"We're going to take your car," they told him. "We're going to paint it for you."

Escalante was not thrilled with their request, which was actually more of a demand than an offer. He loved his little Volkswagen beetle. It was his first investment in America, his first step in a new way of life. It had taken him to jobs as a janitor, a cook, an engineer, and a teacher. He had driven it to night classes at college. Its tiny trunk had hidden the blueprints that helped him begin his climb at Burroughs Corporation. His wife and sons had all learned to drive in it. It had brought him home from the hospital. In twenty years, it had become very comfortable, and he liked its light green color, too.

The young men promised him they did good work and he could trust them. Because of their size and their enthusiasm, he felt he had little choice. He let them take him home and drive off in his beetle.

For almost a week Jaime, Jr., drove his father to school, and Jaime worried about his car. On Friday, true to their word, the pleased body shop workers presented him with his old Volkswagen with a new coat of paint. It was still a light green—with one addition. On the sides were pinstripes, red and blue, the colors of Garfield High.[18]

If it is true that success breeds success, it is also true that success breeds conflict. Very soon after the 1988 release of the film *Stand and Deliver*, a few teachers at the high school, who had long been irritated by some of Escalante's actions and attitudes, began to express their discontent more loudly. Escalante called it jealousy, but several of his colleagues disliked his outspokenness, his curtness, and what they considered his arrogance. "It's the way he acts toward certain people," a fellow math teacher explained, "like he is the master."[19]

Some of the other instructors, especially the Advanced Placement teachers, felt a little resentful that one department and one instructor had received so much publicity when they, too, had made strides with their classes. "There are many of us at this school who are knocking ourselves out and don't get the attention," remarked one English teacher.[20] Besides, the way Escalante worked his students, the kids had little time to devote to A.P. history, physics, or English.

Several counselors had been upset when Escalante circumvented or completely disregarded their advice to his students. They disliked his insistence that he knew what was best for them. They felt he should realize that there were things other than calculus, things other than math, that were important.

The general feeling among a number of people throughout the school was that he had allowed the movie *Stand and Deliver* to "go to his head."[21]

Seated with Jaime Escalante at an awards dinner are Fabiola Escalante (left) and Garfield High's principal, María Elena Tostado (center).

Escalante began to find critical, even threatening letters in his mailbox. Some said he was not wanted any longer at Garfield. He received ugly phone calls from people who would not identify themselves. Some of the callers threatened his life.[22]

In the mathematics department, the teachers who had never understood what Escalante was trying to do with his students became even more disgruntled. They complained about his attempts, as department chairman, to raise standards in the classroom. Many of the students, they insisted, could not handle algebra, much less trigonometry or calculus. He argued that those teachers were teaching grade-school arithmetic. They disliked the way he scheduled classes, reducing the number of lower level courses and teaching most of the advanced subjects himself. They believed they had all helped build a strong math program, but he was the one getting all the credit. They were uncomfortable with his self-assurance and his bluntness.

Some of the unhappy math teachers suggested that Escalante should not remain as department chairman. Escalante felt they ignored the fact that the quality of the programs had improved, that higher-level classes had gained in popularity among students, that record numbers of students were taking and passing the A.P. calculus exam. They focused instead on Escalante's refusal to attend meetings and his reluctance to tend to department mail. He believed some people in the twenty-two-member department simply wanted to block his attempts to improve the quality of math instruction at the school. Whether the motivation was envy, control, or discontent, someone else was elected to chair the department in 1989 and Escalante relinquished the position he had held for eight years.

The vote did not end the discord between Escalante and some of his colleagues. A representative of the teachers' union suggested that he look for another position. The friction intensified even as his impact on students deepened. He reached the point where he "just got fed up with all the mediocrity, the politics, the nonsense, and the lack of appreciation."[23] He would always teach, but he did not have to stay at Garfield. Jaime, Jr., was on his own now, a successful electrical engineer. Fernando had almost finished his civil engineering program at California Polytechnic. It would be no problem to move and start over again. He asked his wife where she would like to live.

Fabiola chose Sacramento. Jaime contacted the largest school district in the city. The superintendent's unhesitating response was: "Welcome! Which school do you want?"

"Which school is the best?" he asked. The superintendent told him.

"Which school is the most difficult?" He described Hiram Johnson, a high school in a working-class neighborhood. In the ethnically diverse school, only six students had passed the Advanced Placement calculus test that year.

"I'll take that one," Escalante said.[24]

He packed up his books, his equipment, and the teaching toys he had made. He sorted through seventeen years of memories. He rolled up all his posters, and, at age sixty, at a time when others think

Jaime Escalante, Jr., became a successful electrical engineer.

of retirement, Jaime Escalante headed for a new city and a fresh challenge. Even if he felt some misgivings about the situation at Garfield, nothing could shake his belief in education or his belief in his students. Once again, he would start from zero. And once again, he was determined to succeed.

When Escalante began his new assignment at Hiram Johnson High School in September, 1991, he found the situation quite different from any he had encountered previously. For one thing, in his seventeen years at Garfield, and in Bolivia before that, his classroom had always been entirely or almost entirely Hispanic. The majority of his students in Sacramento were either European-American (31 percent) or Asian-American (30 percent). He had as many African-American students (19 percent) as Mexican-American (19 percent).[25]

For another thing, he would not be teaching seniors primed for two years to take Advanced Placement calculus. He was to teach freshmen and sophomores. In place of the stimulation of a variety of subjects—algebra 2, trigonometry, math analysis, calculus A and B—he would teach only arithmetic and beginning algebra.

Escalante adapted to the changes. He paired his students carefully so they could help their partners. He obtained a donation of new desks to accommodate this arrangement.[26] He had all his special forms—such as the one in which students agreed to accept a failing

Jaime Escalante in front of a *Stand and Deliver* poster. The poster depicts Edward James Olmos portraying Escalante. Escalante continues to educate and motivate his students to succeed.

grade when they did not do their homework—
translated into Vietnamese as well as Spanish.

Escalante's time-tested techniques remained
unchanged. The same athletic heroes smiled their
encouragement from the walls of the Sacramento
classroom. The same inspiring words hung above the
blackboards. The same sports analogies that helped
unravel the mysteries of higher math for a generation
of Garfield students opened up new vistas of
understanding for Johnson students also. The same
discipline of before-and after-school study sessions
cemented the difficult concepts in their minds.

He saw the same kind of steady progress his hard
work had always netted him. He began a calculus
class his second year at Johnson. He designed and
secured funding for a Saturday math enrichment
program that involved five teachers and included
lunch each week. By 1995, his students were signing
up to receive ten units of high-school credit in the
summer session he had put together at the California
State University, Sacramento campus.

True to the pattern he had followed all his life,
Escalante was not in his new position long before he
found additional activities to fill any empty hours in
his schedule. He plunged into one project designing
calculus workbooks and another producing a written
form of a Public Broadcasting Station television
special he had appeared in with Bill Cosby called

"Math . . . Who Needs It?"[27] He accepted invitations to speak in schools and companies across the state, sharing his insights about how to motivate teenagers. He returned regularly to Los Angeles to help and encourage people working in some of the programs he had helped start. He spent most of each summer teaching in Bolivia, giving back to the country that had given him birth.

Jaime Escalante still does not remember his students' names. He still teases and provokes them into achieving. He still pushes them to their limits, demanding more of them than what they think they are able to do. He still challenges them, by word and example, to live according to the creed that he has proven effective with three generations of high schoolers: Determination + Discipline + Hard Work = Success.

Chronology

1930—Jaime Alfonso Escalante Gutiérrez is born in La Paz, Bolivia.

1940—Escalante family moves from Achacachi to La Paz and Jaime begins school at age nine.

1945— Enrolls in San Calixto High School.

1951— Begins college at Normal Superior.

1952— At age twenty-one, receives first teaching assignment.

1953— Begins teaching at Bolivar High School.

1954— Graduates from Normal Superior.

1954— Marries Fabiola Tapia on November 25.

1954— Begins teaching physics at San Calixto.

1955— Jaime, Jr., (Jaimito) is born on September 27.

1963— Immigrates to the United States.

1964—Wife and son join Escalante in the United States.

1964—Begins working at Van de Kamp's Coffee Shop.

1964—Begins studying at Pasadena City College.

1966—Begins working at Burroughs Corporation.

1969—Fernando is born on July 14.

1973— Receives B.A. degree in math from California State University, Los Angeles.

1974— Receives United States teaching credential and is hired by Los Angeles Unified School District.

1974— Begins teaching at Garfield High School, East Los Angeles.

1978— Teaches first A.P. calculus course.

1981— Elected math department chairman.

1982— Fourteen of eighteen students are accused of cheating on A.P. calculus exam. Twelve students retake the test and all pass.

1991— Begins teaching at Hiram Johnson High School, Sacramento, California.

CHAPTER NOTES

CHAPTER 1

1. Jaime Escalante, Family Math Night address at Firebaugh Middle School, April 7, 1995; *Stand and Deliver,* Warner Brothers, 1988.

2. Personal interviews with Jaime Escalante, March 4 and April 1, 1995.

3. Jay Mathews, *Escalante: The Best Teacher in America* (New York: Henry Holt, 1988), pp. 83–84, 100.

4. Kim Hubbard and David Lustig, "Beating Long Odds, Jaime Escalante Stands and Delivers, Helping to Save a Faltering High School," *People Weekly* (April 11, 1988), p. 58.

5. Escalante, Family Math Night; Interviews with Escalante.

CHAPTER 2

1. Jay Mathews, *Escalante: The Best Teacher in America* (New York: Henry Holt, 1988), pp. 20–21.

2. Personal interviews with Jaime Escalante, March 4 and April 1, 1995.

3 Ibid.

4. Ibid.

5. Mathews, p. 23.

6. Interviews with Escalante.

7. Ibid.

8. Ibid.

9. Ibid.

10. Ibid.

11. Ibid.

12. Ibid.

CHAPTER 3

1. Jay Mathews, *Escalante: The Best Teacher in America* (New York: Henry Holt, 1988), p. 26.

2. Ibid., p. 27.

3. Personal interviews with Jaime Escalante, March 4 and April 1, 1995.

4. Ibid.

5. Mathews, p. 27.

6. Interviews with Escalante.

7. John Gunther, *Inside South America* (New York: Harper and Row, 1966), p. 399.

8. Interviews with Escalante.

9. Ibid.

CHAPTER 4

1. Jay Mathews, *Escalante: The Best Teacher in America* (New York: Henry Holt, 1988), p. 33.

2. Personal Interviews with Jaime Escalante, March 4 and April 1, 1995.

3. Interviews with Escalante; Mathews, p. 34.

4. Interviews with Escalante.

5. Ibid.

6. Ibid.

7. Ibid.

8. Mathews, p. 51.

9. Interviews with Escalante.

CHAPTER 5

1. John Gunther, *Inside South America* (New York: Harper and Row, 1966), p. 397.

2. Ibid., p. 389.

3. Personal interviews with Jaime Escalante, March 4 and April 1, 1995; Kim Hubbard and David Lustig, "Beating Long Odds, Jaime Escalante Stands and Delivers, Helping to Save a Faltering High School," *People Weekly* (April 11, 1988), p. 57.

4. Interviews with Escalante.

5. Ibid.

6. Jay Mathews, *Escalante: The Best Teacher in America* (New York, Henry Holt, 1988), p. 54.

7. Interviews with Escalante.

8. Ibid.

9. Ibid.

10. Ibid.

11. Ibid.

12. Ibid.

CHAPTER 6

1. Jay Mathews, *Escalante: The Best Teacher in America* (New York: Henry Holt, 1988), p. 57; Needham, Nancy, "Meet: Jaime A. Escalante; All He Needs Is 'Ganas,'" *NEA Today* (June 1983), p. 11.

2. Personal interviews with Jaime Escalante, March 4 and April 1, 1995.

3. Ibid.

4. Ibid.

5. Ibid.

6. Ibid.

7. Ibid.

8. Ibid.

9. Ibid.

CHAPTER 7

1. Personal interviews with Jaime Escalante, March 4 and April 1, 1995.

2. Jay Mathews, *Escalante: The Best Teacher in America* (New York: Henry Holt, 1988), pp. 65–66.

3. Ibid., p. 79.

4. Ibid., p. 81; *Stand and Deliver*, Warner Brothers, 1988.

5. Kim Hubbard and David Lustig, "Beating Long Odds, Jaime Escalante Stands and Delivers, Helping to Save a Faltering High School," *People Weekly* (April 11, 1988), p. 58.

6. Mathews, *Escalante: The Best Teacher in America*, p. 83.

7. Ibid., p. 99.

8. Jay Mathews, "Escalante Still Stands and Delivers," *Newsweek* (July 20, 1992), p. 58.

9. *Stand and Deliver.*

10. Mathews, *Escalante: The Best Teacher in America*, pp. 84, 116, 120.

11. Hubbard and Lusti, p. 58.

12. Ibid.

13. Jaime Escalante, Family Math Night address at Firebaugh Middle School, April 7, 1995.

14. Ibid.

15. Nancy Needham, "Meet: Jaime A. Escalante; All He Needs Is 'Ganas,'" *NEA Today* (June 1983), p. 11.

16. Escalante, Family Math Night.

17. Hubbard and Lustig, p. 58.

18. Mathews, *Escalante: The Best Teacher in America*, p. 84.

19. Interviews with Escalante.

20. Ibid.

21. Escalante, Family Math Night.

22. Randy Fitzgerald, "The Teacher They Call 'The Champ,'" *Reader's Digest* (August 1983), p. 119.

23. Ibid.; Needham, p. 11.

24. *Stand and Deliver.*

25. Escalante, Family Math Night; personal interviews.

26. Interviews with Escalante.

CHAPTER 8

1. Randy Fitzgerald, "The Teacher They Call 'The Champ,'" *Reader's Digest* (August 1983), p. 119.

2. Nancy Needham, "Meet: Jaime A. Escalante; All He Needs Is 'Ganas,'" *NEA Today* (June 1983), p. 11.

3. Jay Mathews, *Escalante: The Best Teacher in America* (New York: Henry Holt, 1988), pp. 110–114.

4. Ibid., p. 128.

5. Needham, p. 11.

6. Mathews, p. 125.

7. Mathews, pp. 140–141; *Stand and Deliver,* Warner Brothers, 1988.

8. Jaime Escalante, Family Math Night address at Firebaugh Middle School, April 7, 1995.

9. Mathews, pp. 193–195.
10. Mathews, p. 196; Needham, p. 11.
11. Mathews, pp. 134–135.
12. Mathews, pp. 136–137; *Stand and Deliver*.
13. Mathews, p. 138.
14. Ibid., p. 144.
15. Ibid., p. 152.

CHAPTER 9

1. Personal interview with Jaime Escalante, March 4 and April 1, 1995.
2. Jay Mathews, *Escalante: The Best Teacher in America* (New York: Henry Holt, 1988), pp. 148–154, 164.
3. Ibid., pp. 144, 147.
4. Ibid., p. 149.
5. Randy Fitzgerald, "The Teacher They Call 'The Champ,'" *Reader's Digest* (August 1983), p. 120.
6. Mathews, p. 160.
7. *Stand and Deliver*, Warner Brothers, 1988; Mathews, p. 165.
8. Mathews, pp. 166–167.
9. Ibid., pp. 169–170.

CHAPTER 10

1. Jay Mathews, *Escalante: The Best Teacher in America* (New York: Henry Holt, 1988), pp. 173–174.
2. Nancy Needham, "Meet: Jaime A. Escalante; All He Needs Is 'Ganas,'" *NEA Today* (June 1983), p. 11.
3. Vicky Lytle, "Beyond Elitism: Math Literacy for All," *NEA Today* (November 1987), p. 11.
4. Randy Fitzgerald, "The Teacher They Call 'The Champ,'" *Reader's Digest* (August 1983), p. 122.
5. Charles E. Cohen and Dan Knapp, "Relocate and Deliver," *People Weekly* (September 16, 1991), p. 111.
6. Personal interviews with Jaime Escalante, March 4 and April 1, 1995.
7. Cohen and Knapp, p. 111.

8. Interviews with Escalante.

9. Ibid.; Mathews, p. 217.

10. *Stand and Deliver*, Warner Brothers, 1988.

11. Kim Hubbard and David Lustig, "Beating Long Odds, Jaime Escalante Stands and Delivers, Helping to Save a Faltering High School, *People Weekly* (April 11, 1988), p. 58.

12. Ibid., pp. 57–58.

13. Jay Mathews, "Escalante Still Stands and Delivers," *Newsweek* (July 20, 1992), p. 58.

14. Pat Aufderheide, "Reel Life," *Mother Jones* (April 1988), p. 26.

15. Interviews with Escalante.

16. Hubbard and Lustig, p. 58.

17. Mathews, *Escalante: The Best Teacher in America*, pp. 297–298.

18. Jaime Escalante, Family Math Night address at Firebaugh Middle School, April 7, 1995; *Stand and Deliver*.

19. Cohen and Knapp, p. 112.

20. Hubbard and Lustig, p. 58.

21. Mathews, "Escalante Still Stands and Delivers," p. 58.

22. Cohen and Knapp, p. 111.

23. Ibid.

24. Interviews with Escalante.

25. Mathews, "Escalante Still Stands and Delivers," p. 58.

26. Ibid.

27. Ibid., p. 59.

BIBLIOGRAPHY

Aufderheide, Pat. "Reel Life." *Mother Jones,* vol. 13 (April 1988), 25–26.

Cohen, Charles E., and Dan Knapp. "Relocate and Deliver." *People Weekly* (September 16, 1991), 111–112.

Escalante, Jaime. Family Math Night address at Firebaugh Middle School, Firebaugh, Calif., April 7, 1995.

————. personal interviews, March 4 and April 1, 1995.

Fitzgerald, Randy. "The Teacher They Call 'The Champ.'" *Reader's Digest* (August, 1983), 119–122.

Gunther, John. *Inside South America.* New York: Harper and Row, 1966.

Hubbard, Kim, and David Lustig. "Beating Long Odds, Jaime Escalante Stands and Delivers, Helping to Save a Faltering High School." *People Weekly* (April 11, 1988), 57–58.

Lytle, Vicky. "Beyond Elitism: Math Literacy For All." *NEA Today,* vol. 6 (November 1987), 10.

Mathews, Jay. "Escalante Still Stands and Delivers." *Newsweek* (July 20, 1992), 58–59.

————. *Escalante: The Best Teacher in America.* New York: Henry Holt, 1988.

Needham, Nancy. "Meet: Jaime A. Escalante; All He Needs Is 'Ganas.'" *NEA Today,* vol. 1 (June 1983), 11.

Stand and Deliver. Warner Brothers, 1988.

INDEX